RED AND GREEN

An Appliqué Tradition

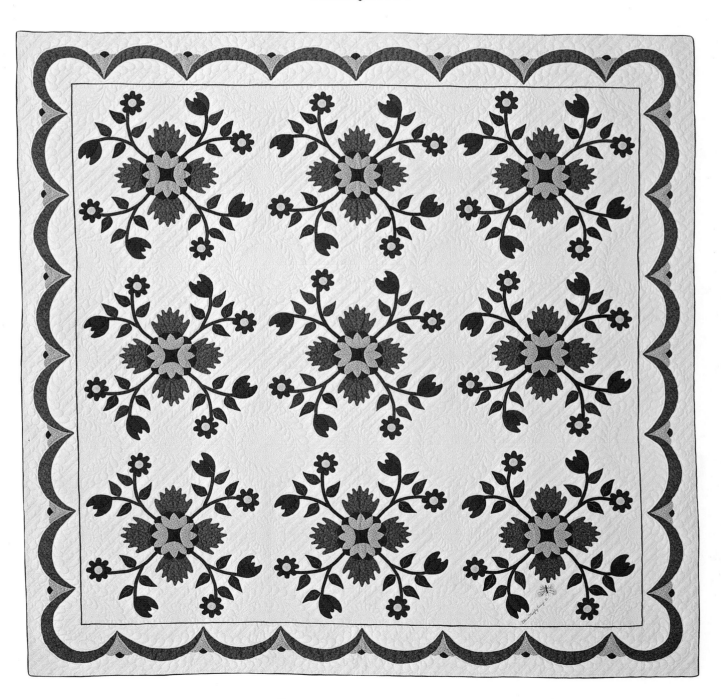

by Jeana Kimball

CREDITS

Photography by Brent Kane (unless otherwise noted)
Illustration and Graphics by Stephanie Benson and Barb Tourtillotte
Text and Cover Design by Judy Petry
Edited by Liz McGehee

Red and Green: An Appliqué Tradition ©
© 1990 by Jeana Kimball
That Patchwork Place, Inc.
PO Box 118
Bothell, WA 98041-0118

Printed in China
05 04 03 02 01 00   9 8 7 6 5 4 3 2

Library of Congress Cataloging-in-Publication Data

Kimball, Jeana
    Red and green : an appliqué tradition / Jeana Kimball.
       p.   cm.
    Includes bibliographical references.
    ISBN 0-943574-68-4 :
    1. Appliqué—Patterns. 2. Patchwork—Patterns. 3. Quilts—United States—History—19th century. 4. Quilters—United States—Biography.
I. Title.
TT835.K489 1990   90-50337
746.9'7—dc20   CIP

(Photo on previous page) Whig Rose, Elline Craig, 1987, Bountiful, Utah, 79" x 79". Elline's remarkable skill with a needle is evident in this beautiful Whig Rose variation. The butterfly in the lower right corner block covers a tiny hole. Elline had just finished her first block and laid it on the floor, when a hot coal popped from the fireplace and landed on her block. She cleverly concealed the hole, and the butterfly gives the quilt added interest. (Collection of Elline Craig)

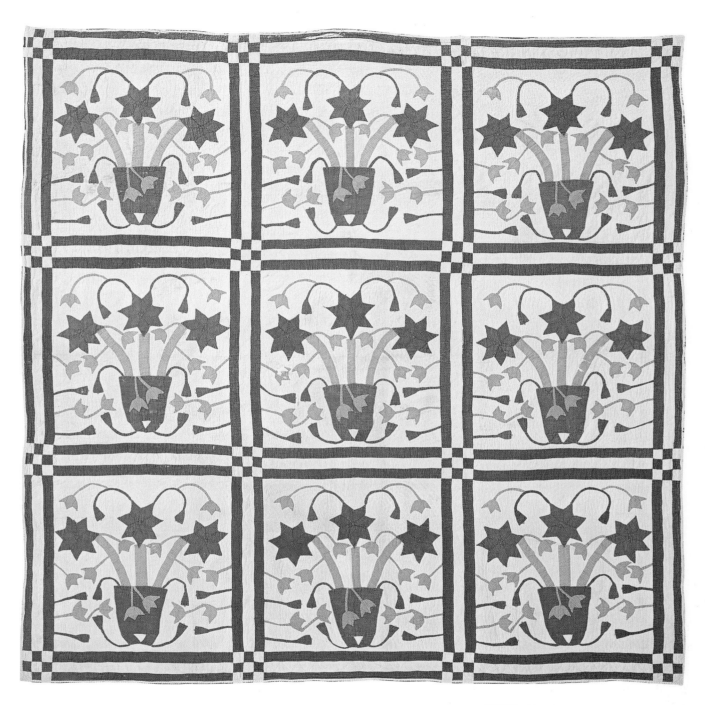

Flower Pot, maker unknown, c. 1850, Pennsylvania. The pots filled with joyful flowers and leaves bring smiles to everyone who views this quilt. You can feel the enthusiasm of its maker, and the pieced border perpetuates the exuberance. (Collection of Judy Roche, Solebury, Pennsylvania)

DEDICATION

To my parents, Ordell and Loraine Hoyt Jones, whose exemplary lives influence and enrich all who know them.

ACKNOWLEDGMENTS

With special thanks to:

Charlie, Nathan, and Emily for their love, support, and help with domestic chores;

Friends and members of my Wednesday Night Quilt Group, who stitched quilts and blocks using patterns from this book: Charlotte Warr Andersen, Maureen Blosch, Annette Bracken, Minerva Colemere, Beth Crawford, Kallie Dent, Kristine Haas, Elna Johnson, and Eleanor Tracy;

Jean C. Christensen for her time, patience, and the use of her beautiful quilts;

Elline M. Craig, Connie Sheffield, Aileen Stannis, and Judy Roche for the use of their wonderful appliqué quilts;

Carolyn Worth for her assistance in obtaining the Oak Leaf and Reel quilt;

Charlotte Pendleton of the Schminck Memorial Museum for generously lending photos, quilts, and biographical information about Elizabeth Currier Foster;

Frances A. Campbell for sharing family photos and biographical information about Nancy Stafford Spoon Shoffner;

North Carolina Quilt Project for transparencies of Nancy Stafford Spoon Shoffner quilts;

Bill Cooke for sharing biographical information, photos, and needlework of Sallie Ann Nelson Edwards;

Nancy Tuckhorn of the DAR Museum for the meticulous data on red-and-green appliqué quilts in the museum's collection and for obtaining photography of four of those quilts;

Marge Conder of the L.D.S. Church Museum of History and Art for arranging and obtaining transparencies of quilts in the museum's collection;

Edith Menna of the Daughters of Utah Pioneers Museum for arranging and assisting when the museum's quilts were being photographed;

Cyril Nelson of E. P. Dutton, Cincinnati Art Museum, Charleston Museum, and Henry Ford Museum for the use of color transparencies.

Contents

Preface 6

The History 7
  The Origins of Red-and-Green Appliqué Quilts 7
  Development of Appliqué 10
  The Colors: Red and Green 14
  Traditional Quilt Formats and Block Sizes 15
  Classic Border Treatment 16

The Makers 17
  Elizabeth Currier Foster 17
  Nancy Stafford Spoon Shoffner 21
  Sallie Ann Nelson Edwards 24
  Dorinda Melissa Moody Salmon Goheen Slade 26
  The Unknown Quiltmaker 28

The Patterns 32
  Rose Designs 37
    Rose Wreath 37
    Whig Rose 44
    Foundation Rose .50
    Diagonal Stem Rose 56
  Other Flower Designs .66
    Tulip 66
    Cockscomb 77
    Prairie Flower and Others 82
  Fruits and Nuts 93
    Berries 93
    Pineapple-Pomegranate 100
    Oak Leaf 109
  Original Designs 113

Borders 124

Bride of Tulip Valley Quilt .125

Gallery 129

Glossary of Techniques 148

Bibliography 157

Notes 159

Preface

Flowers have a timeless quality that is significant to everyone in a different way. Their visual beauty appeals to us all, and the fragrance that accompanies that beauty can bring instant recall in the same way a familiar song brings vivid memories of an event, place, or person from the past. The smell of lilacs reminds me of the first spring with my husband-to-be, sitting on the back porch swing in the moonlight. Rose scents summon visions of me as a small child visiting a rose garden near my home on summer afternoons just to smell the roses and listen to the gurgling fountain. Undoubtedly, you have similar associations.

Women of other centuries also had important relationships with flowers. Elinore Pruitt Stewart, a homesteader in Wyoming, wrote of her special "memory flower bed" in a letter to a friend. (Elinore Pruitt Stewart, *Letters on an Elk Hunt By a Woman Homesteader* [Lincoln, Nebraska: University of Nebraska Press, 1915], 160).

Under the east window of our dining-room we have a flower-bed. We call it our memory-bed because Clyde's [her husband] first wife had made it and kept pansies growing there. We poured the water of my little lost boy's last bath onto the memory-bed. I keep pansies growing on one side of the bed in memory of her who loved them. In the other end I plant sweet alyssum in memory of my baby.

Nineteenth-century women grew flowers and then preserved their beauty by pressing blossoms between pages of a book, making sachets from dried petals, or stitching them into needlework. When stitching her own special "flower quilt," each woman included herself and her memories. Even though she may have used a standard red-and-green appliqué design format, she changed or adapted it to her own liking. Unlike other quilts that she stitched for utility use, her appliqué quilt showed her best side, one that she wanted others to see.

This book has three purposes: to present a summary of historical information about appliqué quilts; to provide traditional patterns and new variations for your use; and to encourage and assist you in the design of your own unique appliqué quilt. Let the flowers you stitch illustrate your personality, your memories, and your best work.

Jeana Kimball

The Origins of Red-and-Green Appliqué Quilts

Needlework in the seventeenth, eighteenth, and nineteenth centuries was probably the most important skill a young girl had to learn.[1] Certainly, basic cooking skills were necessary, but it was also extremely important that she be proficient with a needle. All of the clothing worn by her family, as well as all bedding and furnishings in the home, came from her hands. In 1889, Lucy Larcom described in *A New England Girlhood* her earliest memory of realizing this awesome responsibility:

> I think it must have been at home, while I was a small child, that I got the idea the chief end of woman was to make clothing for mankind. . . . This thought came over me with a sudden dread one Sabbath morning when I was a toddling thing, led along by my sister, behind my father and mother. As they walked arm in arm before me, I lifted my eyes from my father's heels to his head, and mused: "How tall he is! And how long his coat looks! and how many thousand thousand stitches there must be in his coat and pantaloons! And I suppose I have to grow up and have a husband, and put all those little stitches in his coats and pantaloons. Oh, I never, never can do it!" A shiver of utter discouragement went through me. With that task before me, it hardly seemed to me as if life was worth living. I went to meeting, and I suppose I forgot my trouble in a hymn.[2]

At a very young age, girls were trained to use a needle. Mothers taught their daughters to sew early, so they could help with the enormous task of producing and maintaining an entire family's wardrobe and bedding needs.[3] One woman describes her experience of learning to stitch before age three:

> Before I was three years old, I was started at piecing a quilt. Patchwork, you know. My stint was at first only two blocks a day, but these were sewn together with the greatest care or they were unraveled and done over. Two blocks was called "a single," but when I got a little bigger I had to make two pairs of singles and sew the four blocks together, and I was pretty proud when I had finished them and achieved my first "wedding."[4]

By the time a girl reached the age of ten or eleven, she had become quite proficient with her needle. It is said to have been traditional for a young lady to have twelve quilt tops completed and ready to be quilted for her own home by the time she reached marriageable age. Jeannette Lasansky states that surveys in six Pennsylvania counties revealed that four or five quilts were the norm for dowries, rather than twelve.[5] This could be true elsewhere as well. Regardless of the number, it was understood that a young woman would supply the quilts needed to set up her own household. An old verse from England says:

> At your quilting, maids, don't dally,
> Quilt quick if you would marry,
> A maid who is quiltless at twenty-one,
> Never shall greet her bridal sun![6]

It is undisputed, however, that the crowning touch to a young woman's trousseau was the completion of her bridal quilt. This bridal quilt, whether pieced, appliquéd, or a quilted counterpane, was a piece to display the maker's "coming of age" and to demonstrate her skill with a needle. The completion of her wedding quilt showed a young lady's readiness for marriage and mature responsibility. Many finely appliquéd red-and-green quilts were made as bridal quilts.

Red-and-green quilts were not always bridal quilts; they served other purposes as well. My informal survey of documented red-and-green appliqué quilts reveals there are two most common times in a woman's life when she would have made such a masterpiece quilt. One of those times was just before or immediately after her marriage; the other was when the maker reached forty-five to fifty years of age. By this later time in her life, her children were usually on their own, and she had more leisure time to pursue her interests.

Besides the full-size appliqué quilts, there were many lovely baby quilts made in red-and-green appliqué. These pieces were usually based on one large block, with a simple border around the single block. The baby quilts rarely featured stuffed work and usually were not quilted as heavily as the larger quilts. (See page 137 for an example of a red-and-green appliqué baby quilt.)

The old-world tradition of having the best bed displayed in the living room or main entertaining room of the home evolved into having a guest bedroom in the front of the home. "Best" quilts were displayed in the front bedroom and used on special occasions when honored guests were visiting. The kind of quilt covering the bed in the front bedroom was used as a social barometer indicating the importance of the visitor. Ruth Finley tells the story of a newly wedded minister's wife in Kentucky who insisted on accompanying her husband on all of his overnight trips:

> The time of the occurrence was shortly after the Civil War when ministers in that part of the South were still riding circuits. Each was in charge of the congregations of at least four widely separated villages. Such an arrangement took the men away from their homes for days at a time.

> One young minister's wife, contrary to the accepted custom, insisted on accompanying her husband on all of his over-night trips instead of only on very special occasions. Since "preacher" had to be entertained in the homes of his parishioners, this doting bride led to complications, as it was not

always convenient for the busy mistresses of crowded mountain farmhouses or cabins to make the adjustments necessary to entertain the most important couple in the community. Food and a bed were sufficient for "preacher." But when Mrs. Preacher came too, things were different. Not only must the house be scoured from top to bottom before her arrival and extra baking indulged in, but all ordinary work must be laid aside during her stay. It was a custom as old as the hills that the minister's wife must be entertained in second best dresses and white aprons, with hands folded. Two or three times a year this was an honor eagerly sought and greatly enjoyed. Occurring month after month, it was a tax on time and the resources of even Southern hospitality.

The Presiding Elder became much disturbed over a situation which threatened to undermine the prestige of his circuit-rider; already it had led to criticism of the young man as well as his wife. Hints to both did no good, and the reluctant Elder was contemplating plain speaking when his own black-eyed lady took matters in hand.

"It required drastic measures," she explained, "but something had to be done. So I sent word round to all the leading ladies of that circuit not to put their best appliquéd quilts on the spare bed the next time she came, without its being quarterly meeting or a wedding or a funeral when of course she'd be expected. She was pretty headstrong, that girl, but even *she* couldn't ignore what the absence of the best quilt signified."[7]

As families migrated to new parts of the country and set up housekeeping, they were able to take only the most essential items with them. Niceties such as furniture and family heirlooms were left behind. It was possible, however, to justify bringing a best appliqué quilt because it could be classified as bedding. Of utmost importance to the pioneer woman was a link with home, and her appliqué quilt often served in that capacity.

Immediately upon reaching their destination, even before a permanent dwelling was built, the pioneer family planted their garden. Flowers were soon included among the vegetables and grain crops. It was important that their new surroundings feel like "home," and the presence of flowers, like those that had been left behind, gave their new home a feeling of permanence. *Heart Throbs of the West*, a publication by the Daughters of Utah Pioneers, describes how quickly flowering plants were incorporated into the garden: "Many are the stories told of the men going to the canyon to get wood, bringing back a wild rose, a honey suckle root, or a blue bell to transplant in Mother's garden."[8] Whether on a quilt or growing in the yard, flowers served an important role as food for the soul and as a connection with a gentler lifestyle left behind. Today, many western museums and private collections contain fine examples of red-and-green appliqué quilts that were brought west with the pioneers and preserved as an important link with their past.

Regardless of the home in which it was displayed, the red-and-green appliqué quilt brought comfort, pride, and beauty to its surroundings and its owners.

Development of Appliqué

Throughout the nineteenth century, appliqué quilts were the kind of quilt a lady would stitch to showcase her needlework abilities. Whether she was preparing to "come of age" and marry or wanted to have a masterpiece quilt to display on the guest-room bed of her home, the quiltmaker most often turned to appliqué. During the second and third quarters of the nineteenth century, appliqué in colors of red and green was the favorite choice. There were many basic pattern arrangements used, but each quiltmaker added a part of her own personality by varying the design to please herself. A maker's "best" quilt was treasured and carefully cared for during her lifetime and her children's lives, because the appliqué quilt represented a special part of the woman who made it—her very best efforts.

Appliqué work has early beginnings. The Boulak Museum in Cairo owns a ceremonial canopy, dated 980 B.C., that was part of the funeral tent for Egyptian queen Esi-mem-kev. This canopy is decorated with appliquéd Egyptian symbols, including serpents and blossom shapes. These ornamental appliqués are made of gazelle hides that were dyed pink, primrose, bluish green, pale blue, and golden yellow.[9] Later centuries also have surviving examples of appliqué work, including crusader banners and cloaks decorated with appliqué motifs.[10]

The fifteenth, sixteenth, and seventeenth centuries brought more frequent use of appliqué motifs as a substitute for time-consuming crewel embroidery on household furnishings. In the sixteenth century, England began importing fabrics from India, where fine-quality cottons were produced and printed with a dye process superior to the one then known in Europe. As the Indians began to print highly glazed chintz fabrics in colors and designs that suited the European taste, these fabrics became much sought after in European society. Chintz, in both yardage goods and palampores, was sold to the eager Europeans.[11] Palampores were painted hangings comsisting of a large central panel design with elaborate floral borders surrounding it. (See page 11 for an example of a Tree of Life palampore.) The term "painted" was used because painstaking brushwork was involved in the process of applying colors and mordants (substances used to fix the dye) to the fabrics, not because there was true paint present.[12]

Often the theme for the center panel of the palampore was a Great Tree or Tree of Life design with various flowers and birds being featured on, under, and around the tree. This Tree of Life was the most popular theme; other themes included elaborate arrangements of flowers in a circular or medallionlike center. The flowers used on the Indian chintz fabrics and palampores were adapted from traditional European needlework patterns.[13] Palam-

United East India Company Palampore, eighteenth century, 112" x 88". This example of a painted palampore, featuring the familiar Tree of Life theme, was imported from India to England. A narrow band of unpatterned fabric separates the central design from the meandering vine border. (Photo courtesy of The Charleston Museum, Charleston, South Carolina)

pores were used as both hangings and bedcovers.

By the mid-1600s, the use of imported Indian chintz was very popular in both clothing and household furnishings. Alarmed European textile manufacturers demanded that their governments do something to stop this trend that was destroying their businesses. In response, the English and French governments passed laws imposing large tariffs on imported fabrics and even banning their sale.[14] These restrictions made the Indian-manufactured cottons even more desirable and much more difficult to obtain.

The clever European housewife reacted by carefully rationing any chintz fabric she had on hand. A logical solution was to produce her own palampore-type hangings with chintz scraps by appliquéing the cutout flowers and motifs onto a solid background fabric. Many of the quilts stitched in this "broderie perse" technique have a Tree of Life theme. The leftover pieces of chintz were combined with domestic printed and plain fabrics and sewn together into simple pieced quilts.

Later, during the mid-1700s, the Europeans perfected their fabric printing processes and began producing their own chintz fabrics. Use of chintz in household furnishings again flourished and remained popular for many generations.

The emphasis in household decorating during the seventeenth, eighteenth, and early nineteenth centuries was on elaborately embellished counterpanes, bed hangings, and quilts. Continuing into the mid-eighteenth century in America, the master bed was a most important item of furniture and occupied a place of importance in the living room, kitchen, or downstairs master bedroom of the home.[15] Often, the master bedstead was part of the dowry brought by the wife into the marriage and was one of the few items that could remain her property in the event of her husband's death.[16] Since it was the most costly in both time and materials to furnish, as well as a statement of a man's success in choosing a wife, the master bed was a measure of a man's status in his community.

Colonists brought the traditions and techniques of their homelands with them to America. In an effort to make their new homes as comfortable as possible and to echo their former lives, the women worked to duplicate quilts and household furnishings made by their mothers. However, the high cost and scarcity of new textiles made this task almost impossible. Clothing, household linens, and quilts brought with them were recycled as their original uses became no longer practical. Development of new, pieced quilt designs was a logical result of recycling and the need for warm bedding. Appliqué quilts also changed as precious chintz fabrics became impossible for the American housewife to obtain. Flower shapes cut from solid fabric or calico prints were substituted for or combined with motifs cut from chintz on the popular appliqué spreads. (See page 13 for a late-eighteenth- or early-nineteenth-century appliqué counterpane that shows a combination of cutout and chintz appliqué.)

The Revolutionary War brought new changes to the American woman's way of life. The creation of a new country seemed to encourage creativity and independent thinking. Education became more readily available for girls, and clothing styles less confining. The heavy layers of petticoats and corsets were replaced for a time with the new empire-style dress.[17]

Women's role as mother and housekeeper remained much the same, but their new independence showed itself in other ways. It became acceptable for women to attend lectures, the theater, and museums.[18] Appliqué was being used more on "best" quilts, as new and different designs appeared. Each new idea suggested another interpretation to a neighboring quilter, and so appliqué grew.

American-made and imported English chintz fabrics were used in appliqué spreads with the familiar Tree of Life and central medallion themes. However, the new American attitude began an evolution of the way chintz appliqués were used. Designs that

Adam and Eve in the Garden, late eighteenth or early nineteenth century, 55¹/₂" x 45³/₄". Chintz and plain cotton fabrics are combined on this unquilted counterpane. (Photo courtesy of Cincinnati Art Museum, bequest of Mrs. W. M. Simmons, Cincinnati, Ohio)

formerly had been closely placed and busily arranged were now spread out with more background fabric, setting individual motifs apart. The new arrangements gave the spreads an open and less fussy look. This may have been due to the high cost of chintz fabrics, but using more background fabric and sashing between individual blocks also "set off" the pieced designs.

By the early 1800s, a still different look began to develop in appliqué. Calico or plain cutout shapes resembling flowers, stems, and leaves completely replaced the chintz motifs. By 1840, appliqué quilts featuring red-and-green cutout motifs were the favorite type of "best" quilt. For the next fifty years, red-and-green appliqué quilts remained firmly established as the kind of quilt reserved for a lady's most carefully planned designs, her most expensive fabrics, and her best stitches.

The Colors: Red and Green

Almost without exception, during the mid-1800s appliqué quilts were stitched from red and green fabrics on a white or off-white background with only one or two accent colors. These accent colors were typically yellow, pink, and occasionally blue. Strong yellow, pumpkin orange, and an occasional blue were the accent fabrics most frequently found in Pennsylvania and the northern states, while southern quilts favored softer yellows and pinks as accent colors.

Regional areas developed unique trends. One example is the recent identification of several quilts made in Alamance and adjoining counties of North Carolina. These quilts have a distinctive yellow background fabric in place of the usual white or cream color.[19] (See page 22 for an example of a quilt with the Alamance County yellow background.)

The reason for the seldom-varied red-and-green color theme is not completely clear. In Patsy and Myron Orlofsky's book *Quilts in America,* the authors state that mid-nineteenth-century beds were decorated with "accessories of green or crimson harrateen or calico or camlet curtains, valances of chintz or richly embroidered linen."[20] A red-and-green appliqué spread would harmonize very nicely with this arrangement.

Also important was the development, in about 1850, of a new aniline dye that produced a more colorfast product. Green was produced by first dyeing the fabric yellow and then overdyeing it with blue, or by reversing the process. Although the two colors rarely had the same degree of colorfastness, the resulting shade of green was part of the charm in using the overdyed green fabrics. Barbara Brackman surmises, "Green's popularity with mid-19th-century quiltmakers may have been due to its patterns of color loss. It almost always changed color, but in an acceptable fashion."[21] Another new product was "Turkey red" fabric. The term "Turkey" refers to the Mediterranean area of the world and not necessarily the country of Turkey, stemming from the old European idea that any eastern Mediterranean country was part of Turkey.[22] Turkey red was far superior in colorfastness to ordinary red fabric and sold for as much as three times the price of ordinary calico.

Another possible contributing factor to the use of red and green is the common-sense approach that stems and leaves are green in nature and, similarly, roses are often associated with the color of red. Since roses were a favorite flower to use in appliqué quilts, it is not surprising that so many of these quilts had a red-and-green color theme.

More than likely, it was a combination of all of the above factors that led to the tradition of using red and green for "best" appliqué quilts.

Traditional Quilt Formats and Block Sizes

The first appliqué quilts featured a medallion-type design that filled the center section of the quilt. This central medallion was then surrounded by either a pieced or appliquéd border and sometimes a combination of both. Often, the subject for the central medallion was a Great Tree or Tree of Life with either animals or Adam and Eve depicted at its base. (See page 13 for an example of a Tree of Life medallion quilt.) Another popular theme for the center of the medallion-type quilt was a floral grouping, also surrounded by borders.

From 1825 to 1840, the favorite format for appliqué spreads was to break the center section into four separate blocks. These blocks measured from twenty-eight to thirty-six inches square and were stitched together with no sashing between them. The same design was repeated in all four blocks. Often, when the blocks were joined to form the center of the quilt, a secondary design emerged. (See pages 134, 135, and 138 for examples of four-block quilts.) Four-block quilts were usually stitched in red and green fabrics. The counterpane on page 146 is an example of a design that appears to be a four-block design, but, instead, each of the four sections is broken into smaller blocks that are joined to form one of the four major sections. The popularity of the four-block quilt is obvious: the individual sections were easier to handle while stitching than the larger central-medallion type design. Borders were then added to surround, contain, and frame the central design of four-block quilts.

By the mid-1800s, the appliqué quilt was broken down into even smaller units that incorporated sixteen-inch, eighteen-inch, and even smaller square blocks. A factor that may have contributed to the smaller size was the popularity of the friendship quilt at that time. Friendship quilts were sometimes made up of a combination of both pieced and appliquéd blocks. Decreasing the block size of all blocks allowed many people to contribute to the project. These smaller blocks were even easier to manipulate while stitching and soon became the standard size for red-and-green appliqué quilt arrangements.

Red-and-green appliqué "best" quilts were usually stitched together without sashing between the blocks. If sashing was used between blocks, it was usually very narrow so that it would not detract from the bold appliqué designs. Sometimes the blocks were set together with alternating plain blocks so that stuffed work or intricately quilted designs could be featured along with the appliqué.

Carrie Hall tells of one young woman's clever idea for quilting the plain blocks. The prospective bridegroom drew a quilting design for the plain blocks, which the bride carefully stitched herself. ". . . the results were much admired, but no one asked to copy it, as it was understood the pattern was to be destroyed after this one quilt was finished. But the *idea* was copied." Other prospective husbands designed "leaves, linked wedding rings, stars, geometric patterns, fanciful designs, and other original ideas [that] were carried out in the quilting, instead of using conventional designs."[23]

Classic Border Treatment

Classic red-and-green appliqué quilts were usually framed with one large border to allow plenty of room for meandering vines that echoed, enclosed, and complemented the appliqué motifs from the center. The border is the part of the quilt that, in my opinion, tells the most about the maker's personality and how much she enjoyed the appliqué work on her quilt. Even though many quiltmakers derived their quilt blocks from the same basic design, they always treated their borders differently.

Sometimes, the border was a simple, single vine with occasional flowers along it; other borders were very elaborate and used complex arrangements. Sometimes, the borders turned all four corners precisely and equally, while other quilts have a more casual treatment with no two corners being the same.

Occasionally, a quiltmaker would have so many good ideas for her border that all four sides featured different appliqué borders. The Susan McCord quilts on pages 132 and 140 are excellent examples of four-border quilts. Regardless of how each quiltmaker decided to frame her blocks, all the borders are interesting, and each sets the tone for the completed quilt.

Feathered Star with Appliqué Borders, c. 1860, origin unknown, 89" x 83". The pieced feathered star blocks are perfectly framed with an unusual appliqué border. The rich colors are especially appropriate for this quilt's bold design. (Collection of Jean C. Christensen, Salt Lake City, Utah; photo by Borge Andersen)

The Makers

Red-and-green appliqué quilts speak vividly of their makers. From the studied precision used in planning the arrangement (or lack of it) to the unique way a quilt has been signed, each quilt reveals many things about its creator.

As a tribute to nineteenth-century women who stitched red-and-green appliqué quilts, this section includes "spotlights" of a few well-documented quiltmakers with one or more appliqué quilts to their credit. At the end of this section is the story of one beautiful nineteenth-century quilt that was almost destroyed after surviving for 130 years. Its story and detailed description are dedicated to all of the unknown quiltmakers whose work we admire, envy, and try to equal.

Elizabeth Currier Foster

Until her thirteenth year, Elizabeth B. Currier's life had been secure, despite three major moves (from Vermont to Massachusetts to New York and on to Missouri) since her birth. As the youngest of nine children and her mother's namesake, she was probably given special consideration and attention. All of this changed when her mother, Elizabeth, died suddenly of a "flulike" ailment. Her father, Jacob, unable to deal with life without his wife, seemed to give up hope and died a few months later.

This second unexpected tragedy left Elizabeth and her

The Foster home in 1885 with Summer Lake in the background (left). It is situated at the foot of rugged, timbered Winter Ridge (named by John C. Freemont in 1843). Mrs. Foster is standing on the upper porch; James and their youngest daughter, Artie Lulu, are on the lower porch. Portrait is of Elizabeth Currier Foster (1832–1921).

brother, Jacob Manley, age eighteen, orphaned. They turned to their older sister, Sarah, and Sarah's husband, A. L. Humphrey, for assistance. The following spring, in 1846, the four of them decided to make a new beginning for themselves and joined the Applegate Wagon Train bound for the Oregon country. They were the first train to follow the Southern Cutoff, helping to blaze a new trail that would be used by thousands after them.

It is difficult for us to imagine the kind of physical and mental hardships they dealt with daily as they traveled. Death was a constant threat and came from many causes. During the journey across the Black Rock Desert of Nevada, Salita Jane Hendersen, the younger sister of Elizabeth's friend Lucy Ann, died after drinking a bottle of medicine that she had seen the two older girls tasting. Elizabeth felt so bad about the accident that she cut a flower from her treasured beaded bag and left it on the lonely grave. (The beaded bag is on display at the Schminck Memorial Museum in Lakeview, Oregon.)

During an interview in 1914, Elizabeth spoke of her memories of life on the wagon train. "If you consider driving cattle all day, and milking at night when it was so cold you had to warm your hands in the cow's flanks a hardship, that is one we had all the time." Life on the trail was not always a drudgery, though; she also spoke of new experiences and sensations. "We turned off the Oregon Trail at Fort Hall. Before coming to Fort Hall there was a real soda spring. We sweetened some of the water with honey and it foamed up in great shape." She also proudly stated, "Mrs. Humphrey, my sister, and myself were the first white women through Cow Creek Canyon, and my brother, Manley Currier, drove the first wagon through the canyon."

The four finally reached their destination and spent their first winter on Rickreall Creek. The following spring they settled in Benton County, near Corvallis, Oregon. It was while in Corvallis that Elizabeth met and decided to marry James Foster. For their wedding on 30 November 1848, the sixteen-year-old bride borrowed her sister Sarah's wedding dress. The dress was made from white-striped lawn with tiny sprigs of lavendar flowers and berries. Her new husband had come to Oregon a year before Elizabeth on the Steven Meek Wagon Train.

It is believed that the Poke Stalk quilt, on page 19, was stitched by Elizabeth while on the wagon train and after arriving in Oregon. This was probably her wedding quilt. Interestingly, the poke stalk is not a native plant in Oregon. True to nature, Elizabeth stitched the stems on her poke stalk plant in pink fabric; she had obviously become familiar with the poke stalk sometime in her early years.

The newlyweds made their home in Philomath, a few miles west of Corvallis. Oregon became a territory of the United States in 1848 and shortly thereafter, in 1850, the Donation Land Law went into effect. This law provided that any male American citizen over the age of eighteen who settled in Oregon before December 1850 could receive 320 acres of land. His wife could also receive 320 acres. To qualify for ownership, he had to cultivate his claim for four years. The young couple easily qualified for the land, and

Poke Stalk quilt, Elizabeth Currier, 1846–1850, Corvallis, Oregon, 82" x 76". This unusual appliqué quilt was made as a wedding quilt. It is believed that Elizabeth worked on it before, during, and after traveling by wagon train from Missouri to Oregon. The poke stalk plant is realistically depicted, including the pink stems of the plant. (Collection of Schminck Memorial Museum, Lakeview, Oregon)

they worked their farm for many years.

In the early 1870s, they decided to move to a higher and dryer climate for the children's health, since five of their thirteen children had died. They purchased ranch land in the primitive Summer Lake Valley, in Lake County, and once again they were pioneers starting over. Their first home at Summer Lake was a small log cabin, until they built their large frame ranch house that overlooked Summer Lake. Finally, they were building their dream home, and they spared no expense in its construction. Sawed lumber to build their home was purchased at a mill in northern California and hauled by wagon about seventy miles to Summer Lake. To furnish the big house, Elizabeth traveled to Benton County and traded livestock for furniture. She accumulated a wagonload, which her sons hauled over the Cascade Mountains to Summer Lake, approximately three hundred miles. Included with the furniture were an ornate rosewood cabinet-type grand piano and a violin. (These two musical instruments are now owned by the Schminck Memorial Museum.)

An orchard and garden were quickly added to the grounds around the house. Within a few years, the ranch became well known for the fine variety of produce raised there. The Foster ranch also developed a reputation for its superior line of cattle and racehorses.

Another popular commodity of the Foster ranch was hospitality. Their home became a social center in the valley, and an invitation to a "doings" was valued. A large upstairs hall was left unfur-

Rose of Sharon, Elizabeth Currier Foster, 1854, Corvallis, Oregon, 90" x 80". Many of the same fabrics are used in both this quilt and the Poke Stalk quilt (page 19). Note how the secondary flowers were changed to buds on four of the blocks. Also, the lower left block is missing a secondary branch and bud; was it an oversight or intentional? (Collection of Schminck Memorial Museum, Lakeview, Oregon)

nished and was used as a ballroom where dances were held. A wire stretched high across the middle of the room held drapes, and, when a party ended, these drapes were drawn to make separate sleeping quarters for the dancers.

Elizabeth and James had fifteen children, ten who lived to maturity. The four Foster sons followed their father's example and became ranchers. One of them held political offices, and another served on the school board. The daughters all married, some of them better than others. One died in childbirth and two others before they were forty years old. The Fosters' youngest daughter, Artie Lulu Foster Schminck, was the founder of the Schminck Memorial Museum in Lakeview, where many artifacts from the Foster family are kept. All of the children were very handsome and can be seen in family photo albums at the museum.

Elizabeth was a prolific quilter, and the Schminck Museum owns eleven quilts that she made. She enjoyed piecing, as well as appliqué, and made many of both kinds of quilts. Elizabeth approached all aspects of her life with the same enthusiasm and determination shown in her quilts. She enjoyed reading about national and local events and kept her mind sharp and active. In 1921, just a few days before her eighty-ninth birthday, Elizabeth died of natural causes, having lived a long, noble, and productive life.

Nancy Stafford Spoon Shoffner

Single parenthood is a phenomenon that we, in the twentieth century, like to believe is unique to our time. Many women of earlier centuries, however, struggled with similar emotional and economic burdens. Nancy Stafford Spoon Shoffner is one such woman and hers is a remarkable story.

Nancy was born in 1834 in the Snow Camp Community of North Carolina. Her parents, Frederick and Sarah (Moffitt) Stafford, were of English descent and Quaker persuasion. No doubt she was taught many solid Quaker values. As a young woman, she apprenticed to a tailor and used the needlework skills she learned there throughout her life. Her descendants still own many items she made, including the quilts pictured here.

In 1861, Nancy married George Spoon, and they lived on their farm three miles from the village of Alamance, North Carolina. Their son, William Luther, was born the following year.

Not long after the baby's birth, George was called to serve in the Confederate Army. The separation was difficult for both Nancy and George. The family owns a letter Nancy wrote to George beginning with "Dear Companion," in which she spoke of their "babe" and their farm. George never got the letter. He had become a victim of the measles, one of the diseases that plagued Civil War soldiers.

Nancy was heartbroken and desperate, but she wasted no time feeling sorry for herself. She went to work in the fields of her farm more determined than ever to succeed. She later said that the first time she plowed, she was so exhausted she thought she

A back view of the Shoffner farmhouse, Alamance County, North Carolina. Nancy is standing to the right of the buggy, her daughter-in-law, Adeline Neville Spoon, is on the left in the white apron, and Nancy's granddaughter, Nancy Miriam Spoon, is the small child.

Original Design, Nancy Stafford Spoon Shoffner, c. 1850–1860, Alamance County, North Carolina, 88" x 74". The unusual background fabric used on this quilt was also found on other Alamance County appliqué quilts. The serrated edges of the large leaves in the blocks are repeated on the swag border, tying the two elements together to make a lovely quilt. (Collection of Frances Alexander Campbell, Chapel Hill, North Carolina; photo courtesy of North Carolina Quilt Project)

would never make it to the house.

Nancy's nearest neighbor was a large landowner named Michael Shoffner. The elderly Shoffner rode across the creek one day to make an unusual offer to the young widow. Without dismounting his horse he said, "You are killing yourself trying to farm and I need a housekeeper. If you agree to be my wife and run my house, I'll send my workers to farm your land." He also promised to support her and her son and to see that her son was educated. Nancy accepted his offer. After marrying Shoffner, she left her little son on her own farm with her mother and sister and went to live in Shoffner's large house.

Several years later, Shoffner died and left Nancy his house and 147 acres of his land. Records in the Alamance County Courthouse show that Nancy was administratrix for an estate, probably Shoffner's, a highly extraordinary position for a woman during that time and an indication that she had remarkable abilities.

After Shoffner's death, Nancy sold her farm and moved her family (her mother and son) to the larger house. She went back to the fields and struggled alone until her son was old enough to

Cucumber, Nancy Stafford Spoon Shoffner, c. 1850–1860, Alamance County, North Carolina, 86" x 77". This bold design is more widely identified as "Princess Feather." Again, Nancy Shoffner successfully connected a seemingly unrelated border to her quilt by repeating in the border the pieced triangle shapes used in setting the four blocks together. (Collection of Frances Alexander Campbell, Chapel Hill, North Carolina; photo courtesy of North Carolina Quilt Project)

help. The home and 289 acres of land still belong to heirs of Nancy Spoon Shoffner. It is still a working farm, as it has been continuously since Nancy's day.

Her son, Will, received his education after considerable struggle and sacrifice, graduating in 1890 from the University of North Carolina. In 1897, when he was thirty-five years old, he married Addeline Neville of Chapel Hill. They had two children, Nancy Miriam and William Mozart. Among his many positions, the senior Will was surveyor of Alamance County and a federal highway engineer.

Nancy's descendants own several pieced and appliquéd quilts that she made. Since none of them is dated, it is impossible to know exactly when they were made. Along with stitching, she enjoyed other simple pleasures of life. She once said, "What's more pleasure than growing food, cooking, and eating?"

She worked in her garden the last summer she lived. With her son by her side, Nancy died at age seventy-two and was buried in the Mount Pleasant Churchyard. Today Will, his wife, and their two children rest nearby.

Sallie Ann Nelson Edwards

Needlework Sampler, Sarah (Sallie) Nelson, 1848, Benton County, Kentucky, 25" x 8". Twelve-year-old Sallie stitched this sampler (below) while at the Science Hill Academy for Girls in Shelbyville, Kentucky. (Collection of William Cooke, Georgetown, Kentucky). Portrait is of Sarah (Sallie) Ann Nelson Edwards (1836–1922).

Sallie (Sarah) Ann Nelson Edwards was a needlewoman of exceptional ability. The appliqué stitching on her beautiful quilt reflects a degree of difficulty that could only have been successfully achieved by one with advanced needlework skills. All of the appliqué pieces, including the serrated edges of the rose leaves, are expertly turned under and carefully traced with tiny herringbone stitches. The quilting, too, is of exceptional quality: The rose leaves are veined with double rows of quilting stitches to add dimension and detail to this masterpiece quilt. The background is covered with ¼-inch cross-hatching with amazingly small and closely placed stitches. What kind of a person could achieve such excellence?

Sallie Ann Nelson was born on 8 July 1836 in Salvisa, Kentucky. Her ancestors were landowners and possibly merchants in Mercer County, making it possible for her parents to procure the finest education available for their children. At a young age, Sallie was sent to the Science Hill Academy for Girls in Shelbyville, Kentucky. While at the academy, at age twelve, Sallie stitched the needlework sampler shown here. Even at such a tender age, she showed exceptional ability.

In 1860, when she was twenty-four years old, Sallie married William Wilson Edwards. They made their home in Harrodsburg, Kentucky, just sixteen miles from her hometown. One year later, their only child, Loulie M. Edwards, was born.

Even though there is no written record, it is evident that Sallie passed to her daughter the needlework skills she had thoroughly mastered. Several surviving quilts, including an exceptional appliqué quilt and a number of faded and worn utility quilts, reveal Loulie's care and skill.

Sadly, nothing more is known at this time about Sallie and her quilts, although the family continues to research. Sallie's quilt was discovered by her great-grandson, William Edwards Cooke, a few years ago, but unfortunately, his parents had become too feeble to recall details about Sallie or her quilt.

Sallie Ann Nelson Edwards died in 1922 at age eighty-six, but her quilt lives on to speak of her exceptional talent with a needle.

Rose, Carnation, and Pomegranate Bouquet, Sarah (Sallie) Ann Nelson Edwards, c. 1850, Harrodsburg, Kentucky, 94" x 88". The bouquet arrangement of the original design is surrounded by a remarkable vine border that features leaves and flowers from the bouquet. (Collection of William Cooke, Georgetown, Kentucky)

Dorinda Melissa Moody Salmon Goheen Slade

In 1984, I discovered Dorinda and her quilt, Sunrise in the Pines, in a publication by the Daughters of Utah Pioneers. I was fascinated with her quilt and was compelled to learn more about this quiltmaker, whose home in Pine Valley, Utah, had been just forty miles north of where I was born and grew up. Even though there are no longer any of her red-and-green appliqué quilts in existence, I am confident that Dorinda made several, since some of her quilts have appliqué borders. I believe you, too, will be fascinated with the story of this pioneer woman.

Dorinda Slade must have been a true quilting addict. One grandaughter's remembrance supports this statement:

> When I was a girl of thirteen I lived with her during the winter. . . . The high drifts of snow were eight to ten feet deep. One morning she bounded out of her bed, dressed, and with pencil and paper, she sat by the window to draw a quilt pattern from the figures the frost had made. This she called "The Windowpane Quilt." She had on hand as many as nine white bedspreads and thirty-five quilts all designed by her.[24]

She is reported to have made over one hundred quilts in her lifetime—all by hand. "Sewing machines are for lazy people," she answered when asked why she didn't buy a sewing machine.

Dorinda Melissa Moody was born 15 January 1808 in North Carolina. When she was ten years old, her family moved to Alabama. It was in Alabama that she met and married William Salmon at age seventeen. They had three daughters, one of whom died at age two. Her husband's work took him away from home for long periods of time and while on one such trip, he became ill and died. He was buried before Dorinda even got word of his death.

To support herself and her young family, Dorinda sewed for others. In 1835, Dorinda's parents decided to move to Texas, and Dorinda and her two daughters went along. While living in Texas, she met and married Captain Michael Roup Goheen, who was in

The town of Pine Valley (below), as seen from the edge of the cemetery where Dorinda is buried. The white church is recognizable in the distance. The photo (below, right) was taken in the spring of 1989, one hundred years after Dorinda's death. Dorinda spent the last thirty years of her life in the log house on the right. The orchard they planted, the rock walls they built by hand, and part of their log house are still in place. The white church in the center of the photo was built by the first pioneer settlers. To this day, it is still the only public building in Pine Valley. (Photos by Charles Kimball)

Texas as a soldier during the conflict with Mexico. After Michael's release from service, he was given a tract of land in Texas as payment for his military service. Michael was a blacksmith and wheelwright by trade and also managed his own large herd of cattle. During the next nine years, the Goheens prospered, and Dorinda gave birth to four more daughters. Three years later, a son was born.

That same year, in 1850, Mormon missionaries came to the area in Texas where the Goheens lived. Dorinda and Michael were converted and joined the new church. All was going well for the Goheens. However, tragedy struck unexpectedly. Michael was away tending his cattle when he became very ill and died. He was buried before Dorinda knew of his death. For the second time in sixteen years, Dorinda was widowed and left on her own. She turned to her new religion for comfort and strength.

Two years after Michael's death, in 1853, several Mormon families in the area were planning to move to Utah, where church members were gathering to build "Zion." Dorinda decided to make the move, too. By now, her three oldest daughters had married. Her third daughter, Eliza Adeline Goheen Lloyd, and her husband, Robert, also were traveling to Utah. Since Dorinda had freed all of her slaves, she had no one to help her and her four children with the physically difficult tasks of such a long journey.

In the same company traveling to Utah was William Rufus Slade, a widower with seven children. For their mutual benefit, Dorinda and William married, giving them a combined family of eleven children. In July, a disease struck the wagon train, and within a month, Dorinda's only son, young Michael, was dead along with three of the Slade children. The children were buried in shallow graves along the trail.

The Slades arrived in Utah the following year. As with all new arrivals, they were assigned to settle in a particular area of the state where their talents could be put to best use. William and Dorinda were directed to move to southern Utah to help with the cotton and silkworm industries that Brigham Young had planned for that area.

A few years later, the Slades moved to the new Pine Valley settlement, a beautiful valley nestled among the mountains. Pine Valley was a short forty miles from other settlements in arid southern Utah. Pine Valley's primary purpose was to supply lumber to the growing towns of St. George, Washington, and Santa Clara.

The Slades built a four-room log house for themselves with an orchard, a barn, a corral, and a garden. After the orchard matured, William made part of their living by freighting fruit, lumber, and vegetables to a small mining town in Nevada. On one of these trips, he died and was buried before the news reached Dorinda. At age sixty-four, Dorinda had been widowed for the third time.

Quilting was Dorinda's special hobby throughout her life. She sent her quilt "The Whigs Defeat and the Democrat Victory" to the Chicago World's Fair in 1893 and won a fifty dollar prize. In 1897, after Dorinda died, another of her quilts was entered in the Pio-

Sunrise in the Pines, Dorinda Moody Slade, c. 1860–1870, Pine Valley, Utah, 95" x 83¹/₂". This quilt depicts the morning sun shining through pine tree branches. (Collection of the Daughters of Utah Pioneers Museum, Salt Lake City, Utah; photo by Borge Andersen)

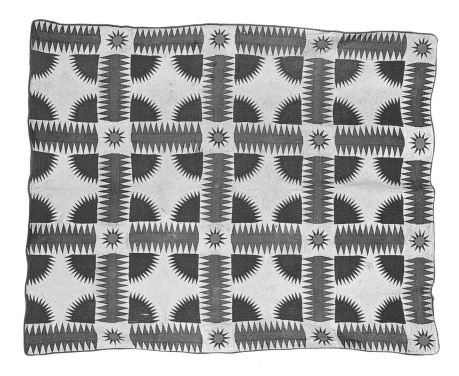

neer Jubilee Fair in Salt Lake City, Utah, where it won first place. All of her quilts reflect her love of quilt design.

Dorinda spent the last years of her life in her tiny log house among the mountains, making quilts and giving them away to friends and family. In November 1895, at age eighty-seven, Dorinda died and was buried in the mountainside cemetery overlooking beautiful Pine Valley.

The Unknown Quiltmaker

The previous stories, which are well-documented accounts of quilters and their work, have been carefully preserved and passed on to each succeeding generation. In too many cases, however, the identity of a quilt's maker is lost and the quilt regarded as a thing of little or no value. Such unwanted quilts are sometimes sold, given away, or used up carelessly and then discarded with no thought to what the quilt represented or meant to its maker. However, on occasion, a quilt is rescued from destruction to be appreciated for what it is and what it represents. The quilt pictured on page 29 is one of the lucky quilts. The story of this quilt and its unknown maker is given as food for thought about quilts you may own or have a chance to study closely. Perhaps you will look at them through different eyes and "read between the lines" about the women who made them.

A few years ago, a woman traveled from Utah to California to assist her grandfather in closing his business, an auto-body repair shop. Since everything was being disposed of, he told his granddaughter that she was welcome to anything on the property of interest to her. Not really expecting to find anything among the mechanics' tools and supplies, his granddaughter took a look

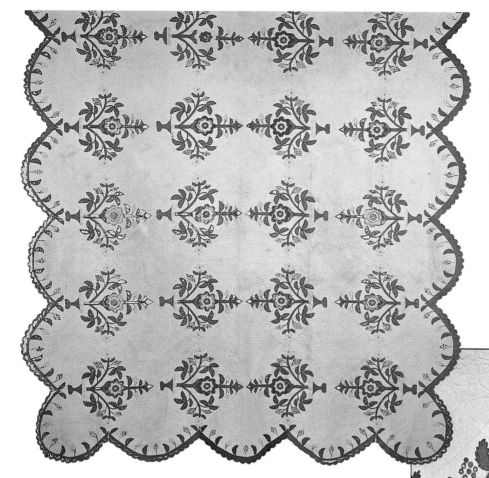

L. R. H. Rose Vase (left), 1858, origin unknown, 100" x 94". Though worn beyond repair, this quilt still speaks eloquently of its maker's skill. In the detail (below), notice the berries, which are stuffed with red fabric trimmings instead of cotton. The even "hairs" stitched along all of the stems give them realism. (Collection of Jean C. Christensen, Salt Lake City, Utah; photos by Borge Andersen)

around anyway. Out behind the garage, in a shed, was a barrel filled with worn clothing and other old textiles. The granddaughter began rummaging through the barrel and underneath an old bedspread she discovered "the quilt." Though she was not a quilter, nor even inclined to sew, there was something about the quilt that, in spite of its worn condition, appealed to her. She removed the quilt from the rag barrel and took it home with her.

Upon her return to Utah, she contacted the only person she knew who was interested in quilts, Jean C. Christensen, of Salt Lake City. Jean, an avid textile and quilt collector, recognized value in this quilt and purchased it from the woman.

At that time, Jean was serving on the board of the L.D.S. Hospital Quilt Show and Auction. She took the quilt to one of the auction's "Quilt Days," where volunteers stitch quilts that are sold at the annual quilt auction. One of the volunteers, Jeanne Huber, was especially taken with the quilt and offered to organize a group to reproduce the quilt for the upcoming auction. Jeanne and several others worked tirelessly for many months to complete a slightly simplified version of this quilt. At the auction in November 1988, the new quilt sold for $10,000.

The old quilt, rescued from its near fate of destruction, had inspired an effort that brought the L.D.S. Hospital in Salt Lake City $10,000, to be used for medical research. What was it about this worn piece of work that motivated so many different people? I believe that, without realizing it, they were all moved not only by the basic design but also by the personal qualities this quiltmaker exhibited in her work. It was the quiltmaker, as much as the quilt, that motivated its reproduction. Close examination of the quilt reveals a wealth of information.

Each of the twenty appliqué blocks and fifteen unusual border blocks is stitched by one person. As you can see from the closeup photo of one of the quilt blocks, the serrated edges of each rose leaf is attached to the background fabric with tiny, evenly embroidered buttonhole stitches. These stitches, placed so closely together, completely conceal the raw edges of the leaves. The stems were first appliquéd with tiny, invisible stitches, and then fine, evenly placed "hairs" were embroidered along each stem to give realism to the appliquéd rose plant.

The outside pink flowers have separate petals that were pieced together and then stuffed as the whole flower was appliquéd to the background fabric. The bud at the top of the block and the upper part of the vase are also expertly appliquéd and stuffed. Many hours and much patience went into making each of the perfectly executed quilt blocks.

The fifty-eight individual berries on each block are also carefully stuffed. (There are 1,704 stuffed berries on this quilt.) In most cases, part of the fabric that was stretched over each of the stuffed berries has been worn off. This wear reveals that several berries on each of the blocks were stuffed with bits of red fabric instead of cotton. This quiltmaker was conscientious about waste and carefully used every scrap of her fabric, including the trimmings.

Surely one so meticulous in her work and fabric usage would not have stitched one of her blocks with the foundation rose in pink fabric in place of red, unless it was meant to be that way. And there it is, on the top row, second from the left, a block with a pink foundation rose. This quiltmaker included an intentional error in her quilt, following the tradition that nothing can be perfect but God.

The twenty blocks were set together "on point" and joined with plain blocks between the appliquéd ones. The alternate plain block allowed a quiltmaker to enhance her quilt by stitching intricate designs between the appliquéd ones, displaying her skill with quilting stitches as well as with appliqué. This quilt layout is common among nineteenth-century quilts. However, the outside border treatment of this quilt is highly unusual. Its maker cleverly avoided the need to construct half and quarter blocks to "square off" the inside of her quilt before adding a long, straight outside border. Instead, she simply rounded one corner of an alternate plain block and stitched it into an outside block position, leaving the rounded corner on the outside edge of the quilt. The "rounded" block was then treated as the outside border of her quilt, appliquéd with a green scalloped swag and embellished with more berries and leaves. The two bottom-corner border blocks were rounded on two sides to make the scalloped border complete. This method of border construction made excellent use of background fabric. Our unknown quiltmaker was ingenious as well as frugal.

The only flaw in the construction of her magnificent appliqué quilt was the miscalculation in the amount of green fabric needed to complete the border appliqué. We can all sympathize with this predicament, since many of us have been faced with the same dilemma. This one unintentional flaw is also appealing because it makes the quiltmaker seem more human in contrast to such perfection in her stitching. The quiltmaker did the best she could to match the green fabric to finish her quilt. Unfortunately, the two greens did not fade in the same way.

The quilt was stitched with four elegant feathered hearts facing the block center on each of the plain blocks, with $3/8$-inch cross-hatching filling in between the feathers and appliqué. Again, the same person hand quilted the entire piece, averaging twelve stitches per inch.

Finally, in her quilting stitches, this unknown quiltmaker revealed one last clue about herself. On the top edge between the two middle blocks (where it would be hidden by pillows), using red thread, she quilted her initials and the date, "L.R.H. 1858."

We know that L.R.H. finished this beautiful piece in 1858, and we can speculate that it was stitched as a bridal quilt because of the heart theme in the quilting. In the nineteenth century, it was considered extremely bad luck to quilt hearts into any quilt other than a bridal quilt. Rings and hearts symbolized love and marriage. In a society where marriage was virtually a woman's only goal, a heart motif was never used lightly.

In summary, we know that L.R.H. was an excellent seamstress with infinite patience; she was also very frugal. Her appliqué design is a one-of-a-kind arrangement, and her method for border construction extremely ingenious, both of which speak of an artistically talented and bright woman. The method and placement of her signature on the quilt suggests modesty as another of her attributes. It is no wonder that L.R.H.'s quilt, speaking through 132 years, is still bringing her the admiration she richly deserves.

A slightly modified pattern is provided on page 119 for those who would like to reproduce L.R.H.'s wonderful quilt.

The Patterns

Appliqué offered a design freedom to women of the nineteenth century, at a time when they were gaining freedom in other aspects of their lives as well. The industrial revolution brought factories and many jobs, which, in turn, caused a large immigration movement to the United States. Inexpensive servants became available, and women who had them were freed from the drudgery of many household chores. They had more leisure time with which to pursue genteel occupations. An added innovation was the development and availability of the sewing machine for household use. The sewing machine speeded up the process of clothing and household linen production, giving women still more time to lavish stitches on their favorite hand-sewing projects.

Because appliqué presented a variety of design possibilities, it was a natural choice for a quiltmaker planning her masterpiece quilt. This best of all her quilts needed to be original and represent her to those viewing her work. Unlike piecing, appliqué had no rules or required formats for putting together a design; the only limitations were the size of the background fabric and the maker's imagination. Appliqué was also appealing because elements from several sources could be combined to create a new design.

Many of the floral elements found on appliqué quilts are also found in designs used in crewel embroidery and on chintz fabrics. It is not possible, for example, to follow the evolution of a design from its origins in a crewel spread into the form used in a red-and-green appliqué quilt, but the use of similar shapes and the same elements suggests that appliqué was influenced by motifs used in other mediums accessible to the quiltmaker.

Since designs were so freely mixed and interchanged, it is difficult to put a name on any one particular design. Even when a basic plan or format was followed, such as a Whig Rose, each maker varied and individualized the traditional design to create her own variation, thus making endless versions based on a single idea. In fact, it is rare to find two appliqués that are exactly alike.

Just as a quiltmaker freely arranged her appliqué pattern, she also freely chose its name. Consequently, a design that is commonly known as "Whig Rose" could just as easily have been named "Rose of Sharon" by its maker. These name variations create numerous complications when trying to categorize appliqué patterns by name.

DESIGN CATEGORIES

In an effort to organize and identify the designs in this book, I have placed them into general design categories. The designs chosen were taken from red-and-green appliqué quilts that repeated the same one or two blocks throughout the quilt. Red-and-green appliqué work in album quilts, where each block is different, were not included in this survey of patterns. The categories are as follows:

1. **Rose Designs.** This includes quilts that incorporate roses as the major design element of the block. I have defined "rose" as a round flower with scalloped, petallike edges. Also, for a pattern to fit into this category, the same general arrangement of the blocks must have been found on at least two to three different quilts. If not, it was placed in the Original Designs category.
2. **Other Flower Designs.** This category includes tulips (the second most common flower design) and other distinctive flower shapes. Again, the same flower or block arrangement was found on at least two to three different quilts.
3. **Fruits and Nuts.** Included in this category are patterns that feature foliage, fruits, or nuts as the major focus of the block.
4. **Original Designs.** The quilts in this category are "one-of-a-kind" designs that consist of unusual arrangement and design elements.

Each of the design categories begins with sketches of several versions of patterns from that category. When possible, each sketch is accompanied with a listing of the source of the design. The sketches are presented as an aid in planning and designing your own unique version should you choose to do so. The reference allows you to go to the original source to closely examine the complete quilt for further ideas on color, block arrangement, and borders. The designs in this book, both full-size and sketched, are not meant to be a comprehensive source of designs; rather they serve as a guide to give an overview of the most common types. Not included in this collection are Princess Feather or Eagle patterns. Many examples and variations of both these designs were found, but the patterns presented here are limited to plant themes.

PLANNING

There are twenty 16" blocks, three 12" blocks, one 32" block, and one complete quilt (including border) found in this book, allowing many options for quilt designs. Additionally, many sketches are given at the beginning of each design category for more examples of block variations. By using the pattern drafting instructions provided in the Glossary of Techniques on pages 149–51, you can design your own unique version, should you choose.

The size of your finished quilt is flexible, since you can choose the number of designs or repetitions you use. You can easily plan a small wall hanging or baby quilt. Choose any one of the full-size blocks provided and center it on a 33" square or larger piece of background fabric. The 32" block (pattern on pages 104–6) would also make a lovely wall or baby quilt. If a four-block quilt is appealing to you, simply cut the background fabric larger (33" or more) and repeat the 32" block pattern (or one of your own designs) three more times and add a border of your choosing. See the Gallery on pages 129–47 for examples of small quilts, both old and new, and four-block quilts.

An appliqué sampler would also be lovely as either a wall hanging or a full-size quilt. Two appliqué samplers made from the patterns in this book are shown on pages 129 and 133.

The Baltimore Album–type block patterns given in my first book, *Reflections of Baltimore,* are also based on a 16" block and can be combined with blocks from this book, should you choose.

The appliqué instructions for the twenty 16" patterns suggest that background fabric for each block be cut 20" square. After appliqué is complete, cut the background 16½" square before joining blocks and borders. Should you decide to leave the background larger, be sure to make allowances for increased size when joining the blocks and borders.

There are endless possibilities for appliqué quilt settings and borders. It is hoped that you will use this book as a starting point to begin your own design adventure.

COLOR

Red and green were used as the major color theme for masterpiece appliqué quilts in the nineteenth century, and the use of these two colors has become synonymous with classic appliqué. As a twentieth-century woman, you have unlimited possibilities for color choices and should choose your fabric colors to suit yourself. The ladies who stitched samples for this book used the traditional theme of red and green, but with variations using other shades and colors as well. See the Gallery on pages 129–47 for the variations they used.

CONSTRUCTION

Construction of the quilt blocks contained in the pattern section is completed in the following steps. Read this section before beginning work on any of the blocks to allow better use of the patterns provided.

1. **Master Pattern.** Fold a square paper the size of your finished block into fourths; this will make it easy to line up pattern sections. Carefully trace the sections of the pattern onto this square piece of paper. This step creates a Master Pattern to refer to as work progresses. A diagram, showing how the individual pattern pages overlap, is given with each block. Mark the design dark enough to allow the Master Pattern to be visible when the background fabric is placed over it.

2. **Making Templates.** Using plastic template material, trace and cut each template pattern piece the actual size, as it appears on the Master Pattern. Occasionally, a pattern piece will be used only once or twice in the construction of the block; use paper templates for these limited-use pieces. An easy way to make paper pattern templates is to photocopy the Master Pattern and cut it apart into individual pattern pieces.

3. **Fabric Selection.** Appliqué is most successful when 100% cotton fabric is used. Cotton turns under more easily and stays

in place more readily than synthetic fabrics. A combination of solid and print fabrics is recommended to add interest and texture.

4. **Marking and Cutting.** Before making your first block with any of these patterns, mark, cut out, pin, and arrange your fabric pieces on a separate piece of paper or fabric (apart from your background fabric). This "pin-up" gives you the option to change your mind and rearrange colors or fabrics, so that the final product will please you.

Each piece is marked on the right side of the fabric for needle-turn appliqué. (See Glossary of Techniques on pages 151–54 for a detailed description of needle-turn appliqué.) Mark each pattern piece by accurately tracing around the template, being sure to make a clear, sharp line. A mechanical pencil is preferred for marking because it gives a sharp, accurate line. On dark fabric, a silver- or yellow-colored pencil is recommended.

Using a sharp pair of scissors, cut out each piece 3/16" from the marked pencil line. A seam allowance that is too wide causes lumpy edges, while one that is too narrow will fray easily.

5. **Background Fabric Preparation.** Most of the quilt blocks in this book are 16" square (finished). For each 16" block, cut fabric 20" square. The excess fabric can be trimmed after the block is completed, if desired. Occasionally, during stitching, the pieces slip and the design shifts slightly as work progresses. By trimming after the appliqué is finished, you can "center" the design by trimming more fabric from one or two sides.

Each pattern has dotted lines indicating the center (and sometimes, diagonal) lines (see Master Pattern on page 34). Be sure these center lines are indicated on each Master Pattern. Prepare background fabric by folding in fourths (fold in half and then in half again). Press fold lines. Unfold background fabric and lay it over the Master Pattern. Pin center of fabric to center of pattern. Line up pressed folds with Master Pattern folds; pin. The Master Pattern is now lined up squarely with background fabric.

To mark background fabric for placement of appliqué pieces, trace lightly 1/4" inside the design. By marking 1/4" inside actual placement, you allow extra room for shifting as appliqué progresses, and you also keep the appliqué placement markings hidden.

Appliqué Hints: Applique pieces are stitched onto background fabric similar to the way a plant grows: first the stem, second the leaves and buds, and finally the flowers. Follow this general rule when determining the order in which to appliqué the pieces. Refer to the Master Pattern while appliquéing to ensure correct order of placement.

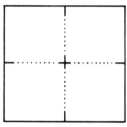

Mark center lines

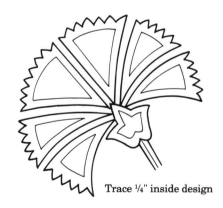

Trace 1/4" inside design

EMBROIDERY

Use two or three strands of good-quality embroidery floss and small embroidery needles. The smaller the needle, the finer the stitch you will achieve.

Following the appropriate stitch diagrams, make small, accurate stitches. Refer to pattern pages and color photos for placement of embroidery. (Embroidery detail is optional and may not appear on color photo.)

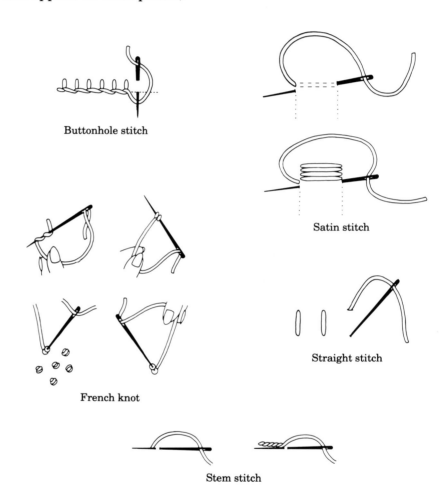

Buttonhole stitch

Satin stitch

French knot

Straight stitch

Stem stitch

Rose Designs

Roses are representative of love, and that symbolism has continued throughout countless generations with the same enduring message. It is, therefore, understandable that "rose" quilts were most often wedding quilts.

Regardless of the design arrangement, wedding quilts were often christened "Rose of Sharon." The title was inspired by the most famous of all love songs, the biblical Song of Solomon 2:1–3:

> I am the rose of Sharon, and the lily of the valleys. As the lily among thorns, so is my love among the daughters.

> As the apple tree among the trees of the wood, so is my beloved among the sons. I sat down under his shadow with great delight, and his fruit was sweet to my taste.

By simply christening her quilt "Rose of Sharon," the proper nineteenth-century lady could express her most romantic feelings without actually verbalizing all of what the biblical lyrics so graphically describe.

Another sure sign of a wedding quilt was the use of heart shapes in the quilting. Ruth Finley, in *Old Patchwork Quilts and the Women Who Made Them,* states that before 1840 the heart was reserved for the bride. To use the heart shape in any other quilt was unlucky and could cause the most dreaded disaster—a broken engagement.[25]

The favored rose was incorporated into many arrangements. There are, to name a few, the "Rose Wreath," the "Whig Rose," "Rose Tree," and various state-named roses, such as "Ohio Rose," "California Rose," etc.

Rose Wreath

One of the most commonly used rose designs is the Rose Wreath. It is identified by many different names, such as "Garden Wreath," "President's Wreath," or "Dahlia Wreath." Almost without variation, the Rose Wreath includes four roses, four or more buds, and as many leaves as necessary to fill in the circular vine between flowers and buds. The four roses are placed at equal intervals along the vine with the buds between them. Occasionally, a fifth rose is added in the center of the circle created by the vine. There are two different full-size Rose Wreath patterns on pages 40 and 42–43. Also provided are sixteen sketched versions of the Rose Wreath to inspire you to design other Rose Wreath variations (see page 38).

ROSE WREATH SKETCHES

1. Bettina Havig, Missouri Heritage Quilts, p. 20; 2. Marsha McCloskey, Christmas Quilts, p. 25; 3. Ruth E. Finley, Old Patchwork Quilts and the Women Who Made Them, *Plate 4; 4. Finley,* Old Patchwork Quilts and the Women Who Made Them, *Plate 27; 5. Carleton Safford and Robert Bishop,* America's Quilts and Coverlets, p. 166; 6. private collection; 7. Lady's Circle Patchwork Quilts *(Spring 1983), p. 15; 8. Marsha McCloskey,* Christmas Quilts, p. 24; 9. Robert Bishop *and Carter Houck,* All Flags Flying, p. 18; 10. Sandi Fox, Small Endearments, p. 33; 11. Safford and Bishop, America's Quilts and Coverlets, p. 167; 12. Barbara Brackman, American Patchwork Quilt, *Plate 11; 13. Sandi Fox,* 19th Century American Patchwork, *Plate 13; 14.* Quilting USA, *No. 9, p. 10; 15. Jeannette Lasansky,* Pieced By Mother, pp. 58–59; 16. Brackman, American Patchwork Quilt, *Plate 10.*

CONSTRUCTION

1. Use the single pattern section on page 40 to make Master Pattern. First, trace the design onto the lower right section. Next, fold Master Pattern in half horizontally and trace upper right section. Refold vertically and trace left side of block, completing the wreath.

2. The vine can be constructed in one of two ways: (a) use separate pattern pieces for each stem section, appliquéing the four stem pieces first before stitching roses, buds, or leaves; or (b) cut a bias strip that is ³⁄₈" wide (finished width) and 18" long. (See Bias-Strip Construction on page 155.) When using the bias-strip method, cut bias strip into four 4½" sections and appliqué them separately. Leave an ample raw edge to fit under overlapped rose petals. Since the rose is an open design, the stem cannot continue underneath rose to next stem.

3. Appliqué roses, beginning with hexagon in the center and building out in rows around the center. Complete the yellow row of petals next and the red row of petals last. Slight adjustments while stitching may be needed to leave "air" between the petals.

4. Stitch the buds and leaves. Reverse appliqué on buds is optional. (See instructions for Reverse Appliqué on pages 155–56.)

BLOCK No. 1
Hexagon Rose Wreath

Finished Size: 16" x 16"

Several years ago, when I first began stitching quilts, I was charmed by the rose in the Hexagon Rose Wreath. During a visit to the Daughters of Utah Pioneers Museum in Salt Lake City, I spotted a red-and-green quilt that used this hexagon-based rose in an asymmetrical arrangement. That quilt, stitched by Elizabeth Shank of Rogerville, Ohio, in 1842, is shown on page 141. I later found another almost identical quilt (*America's Quilts and Coverlets* by Carleton Safford and Robert Bishop, p. 184) titled "Rose of Sharon," which was made in Vermont about 1850. A rose based on a hexagon is unusual, and it inspired me to design my own quilt. I took the hexagon rose from the asymmetrical setting and placed it in a symmetrical wreath setting. Also appealing to me was the secondary design created when the blocks were stitched together. I cut the background fabric for my four-block quilt 27" square and appliquéd a hexagon rose in each corner. When the four blocks were stitched together, I added stems and leaves to complete the secondary design. My Hexagon Rose Wreath quilt can be seen on page 134.

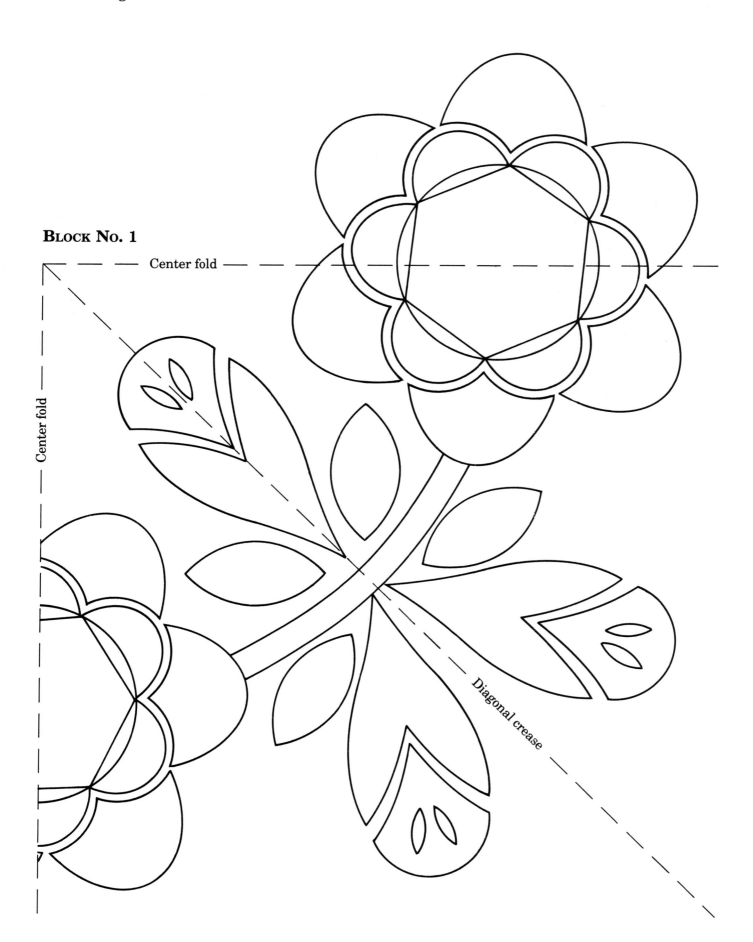

BLOCK NO. 1

Center fold

Center fold

Diagonal crease

BLOCK NO. 2
Single Rose Wreath

Finished Size: 16" x 16"

The simplicity of this single rose wreath makes it appealing. The rose features reverse appliqué cutout petals that reveal the secondary pink fabric. The cutout rose is an effective nineteenth-century variation used to add dimension to an otherwise plain flower.

CONSTRUCTION

1. Trace the two pattern sections (bottom and top), found on pages 42 and 43, onto one-half of Master Pattern. Fold Master Pattern in half vertically and use a light box or window to trace the mirror image on other side to complete pattern. (See page 156 for light box suggestions.)

2. The main vine and secondary bud stems are all cut out as one large piece. By cutting the stems all in one piece, you will save the time required to cut out and stitch each secondary bud stem separately. Fabric scraps left from cutting out this large piece can easily be used up when cutting out the individual leaves.

   Baste vine to background fabric along center of main vine. Beginning stitching at top of block, insert and complete each bud appliqué just prior to appliquéing the stem that encloses it. Work around the inside of the wreath first and then the outside. The leaves can be added as you go or after the vines and buds are finished.

3. Appliqué the rose. (Directions for Reverse Appliqué used on the cutout petals and rose center are on pages 155–56.) The yellow fabric for the rose center is placed between the red and pink fabrics prior to stitching the rose to the background.

Cut out in one large piece

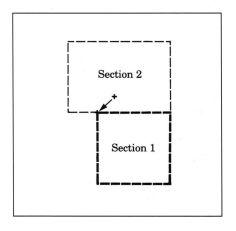

Section 2

Section 1

BLOCK NO. 2
SECTION 1

Center fold

Center fold

BLOCK NO. 2
SECTION 2

Center fold

Center fold

WHIG ROSE

Political issues were a prominent topic discussed among nineteenth-century women. In a smaller population, individuals were more personally and directly affected by political decisions, and a single vote carried much more weight than today. Even though they were not allowed to vote, women could and undoubtedly did influence those who were able to vote.

Many quilt patterns were named after political parties, presidents, and campaign slogans. The name "Whig Rose" is one that caused considerable controversy. Ruth Finley, in *Old Patchwork Quilts and The Women Who Made Them,* says:

> There was the "Whig Rose," the "Democrat Rose," the "Harrison Rose" and a "Mexican Rose," all very much alike, so much alike, in fact, that at one time a controversy was waged to determine to which political camp this general rose design originally belonged. The Whigs claimed it, and the Democrats claimed it, and the dispute was never settled.[26]

It does seem that the Whigs won since that is the name most often associated with this rose design.

The Whig Rose follows a fairly rigid format. There is always a large center rose made up of various layers. Attached to the center rose are four large, green flange sections. Four stems coming from under the rose fit between the green flange sections and then curve around each flange. There is usually a smaller rose and bud arranged on each stem. (See Whig Rose sketches on page 45 for variations.)

WHIG ROSE SKETCHES

1. *Robert Bishop,* Quilts, Coverlets, Rugs and Samplers, *Plate 162; 2. Jonathan Holstein and John Finley and,* Kentucky Quilts 1800–1900, *p. 70; 3. Ruth E. Finley,* Old Patchwork Quilts and the Women Who Made Them, *Plate 19; 4. Carleton Safford and Robert Bishop,* America's Quilts and Coverlets, *p. 162; 5. Sandi Fox,* 19th Century American Patchwork, *p. 14; 6. Finley,* Old Patchwork Quilts and the Women Who Made Them, *Plate 64; 7. Jeannette Lasansky,* In the Heart of Pennsylvania, *p. 6; 8. Cyril I. Nelson and Carter Houck,* The Quilt Engagement Calendar Treasury, *p. 13; 9. Sandi Fox,* Small Endearments, *Plate 37; 10. Karoline Patterson Bresenhan and Nancy O'Bryant Puentes,* Lone Stars, *pp. 56–57; 11. Safford and Bishop,* America's Quilts and Coverlets, *p. 163; 12. Cyril I. Nelson and Carter Houck,* The Quilt Engagement Calendar Treasury, *p. 162; 13. private collection; 14. Fox,* Small Endearments, *p. 33; 15. Robert Bishop,* New Discoveries in American Quilts, *p. 76; 16. Sandi Fox,* Quilts in Utah, *p. 24.*

BLOCK NO. 3

Traditional Whig Rose

Finished Size: 16" x 16"

This Whig Rose is typical of the majority of appliqué blocks with this name. The fabric colors are also very traditional. Eleanor Tracy used a different color arrangement of this block in her Red and Green Garden quilt (page 129), giving it a different but appealing look. Another version of this block was made into a wall quilt by Maureen Blosch (page 135). Note Maureen's unusual, yet effective, border treatment.

CONSTRUCTION

1. Use the single pattern section on page 47 to make Master Pattern. First, trace the design onto the lower right section. Next, trace the pattern onto the uper right section; continue tracing the pattern in a counterclockwise direction around the Master Pattern. If the paper slips slightly while tracing the center rose and its various layers, make adjustments as necessary: use a compass to make the circles round, etc.
2. The stems and large flange sections must be stitched first before appliquéing the center rose. The smaller rose and leaves can be added any time after the stems are complete.
3. The center rose is appliquéd, not pieced, in the following order:
   a. Large outside scalloped rose. After appliqué of this rose is complete, cut away the background fabric. (See instructions for Cutting Away Back of Appliqué on page 154.) After each layer of the rose is completed, the previous layer should be cut away where it is overlapped. This will reduce the bulk produced by several layers.
   b. Dogtooth rose layer. Make adjustments as necessary while appliquéing to be sure the sharp outside points touch the "valleys" between scallops of the first layer.
   c. Smooth circle layer. Again, make adjustments as needed while stitching to make sure the outside edge of this layer "skims" the "valley" points of the dogtooth rose.

d. Small scallop rose (center). Before beginning to stitch this fourth layer, prepare it for reverse appliqué by placing flower center fabric between it and the previous circle layer. (See Reverse Appliqué instructions on pages 155–56.) After it has been appliquéd, use reverse appliqué to finish the flower center.

BLOCK No. 3

BLOCK NO. 4
Complex Whig Rose

Finished Size: 16" x 16"

This Whig Rose is a little more challenging than the Traditional Whig Rose, but the finished result is well worth the extra effort. This design could easily be enlarged to make a lovely wall hanging by redrafting it with methods shown on pages 149–51.

CONSTRUCTION

1. Use the single pattern section on page 49 to make Master Pattern. First, trace the design onto the lower right section. Next, fold Master Pattern in half horizontally and trace upper right section. Refold vertically and trace left side of block, completing pattern. If the paper slips slightly while tracing the center rose and its various layers, use a compass to make necessary adjustments.

2. The stems and large flange sections must be stitched first before appliquéing the center rose. Appliqué the buds along with the stem. The smaller rose and leaves can be added anytime after the stems are complete. Appliqué layers of smaller rose in same order as described for center rose, below.

3. The center rose is appliquéd in the following order:
   a. Outside scalloped rose. After appliqué of this rose is complete, cut away the background fabric. (See instructions for Cutting Away Back of Appliqué on page 154.) After each layer is complete, the overlapped previous layer should be cut away to reduce the bulk produced by several layers.
   b. Second circle layer. Center and appliqué, keeping edges smooth and round.
   c. Inverted four-point layer. Before beginning to stitch this third layer, prepare it for reverse appliqué by placing flower center fabric between it and the second circle layer.

(See Reverse Appliqué instructions on pages 155–56.)
Arrange the four points so that they are divided equally
between three scallops of the first layer of this rose, as
shown in the color photo. After rose has been appliquéd,
use reverse appliqué to finish the flower center.

BLOCK No. 4

Center fold

Diagonal crease

Center fold

FOUNDATION ROSE

This basic rose format is the one most often associated with the "Rose of Sharon" title. Its appeal to nineteenth-century quiltmakers was the limitless possibilities it offered. Beginning with a simple rose in the center of the block, endless variations in the placement of vines, buds, and leaves are possible. Even the foundation rose itself offers much variety. Sometimes the center rose is very large and complex, leaving room for only a few leaves and buds. Other historical examples display a smaller, simpler foundation rose with the stems and buds being the focal point of the block. Sketches of both types of foundation rose blocks are shown on page 51.

Another name occasionally given the larger center rose–type block is "Whig Rose." This basic arrangement differs greatly from the traditional Whig Rose format. The use of the Whig Rose name with this design arrangement is further evidence that names were chosen freely by the makers or their families, regardless of the basic format.

You are encouraged to use the two full-size patterns and sixteen sketches given here as a beginning to design your own unique version of the Foundation Rose.

FOUNDATION ROSE SKETCHES

1   2   3   4

5   6   7   8

9   10   11   12

13   14   15   16

1. Marsha MacDowell and Ruth D. Fitzgerald, Michigan Quilts, 150 Years of a Textile Tradition, *p. 41; 2. Bettina Havig,* Missouri Heritage Quilts, *p. 72; 3. Jonathan Holstein and John Finley,* Kentucky Quilts 1800–1900, *p. 36; 4. Holstein and Finley,* Kentucky Quilts 1800–1900, *p. 49; 5. Carrie A. Hall and Rose G. Kretsinger,* Romance of the American Patchwork Quilt, *p. 112; 6. Carleton Safford and Robert Bishop,* America's Quilts and Coverlets, *p. 169; 7. Robert Bishop,* Quilts, Coverlets, Rugs and Samplers, *p. 165; 8. Barbara Brackman,* American Patchwork Quilt, *Plate 44;*

9. Carrie A. Hall and Rose G. Kretsinger, Romance of the American Patchwork Quilt, *p. 108; 10. Marsha McCloskey,* Christmas Quilts, *p. 29; 11. Nancy J. Martin,* Pieces of the Past, *p. 26; 12. Safford and Bishop,* America's Quilts and Coverlets, *p. 169; 13. Bets Ramsey and Merikay Waldvogel,* The Quilts of Tennessee: Images of Domestic Life Prior to 1930, *pp. 11, 45; 14. Safford and Bishop,* America's Quilts and Coverlets, *p. 168; 15. Ramsey and Waldvogel,* The Quilts of Tennessee, *pp. 7, 8; 16.* Lady's Circle Patchwork Quilts, *No. 23 (1981), p. 26.*

BLOCK NO. 5
Basic Foundation Rose

Finished Size: 16" x 16"

The simple shapes and arrangement of this block make it an excellent choice for your first appliqué. Should you want to vary the center rose, you can easily substitute one of the other rose designs from this book in place of the two innermost rose motifs. Experiment with different variations on a separate paper from your Master Pattern until you find a combination that pleases you.

Center rose from Whig Rose pattern has been substituted for simple center rose

CONSTRUCTION

1. Use the single pattern section on page 53 to make Master Pattern. First, trace the design onto the lower right section. Next, fold Master Pattern in half horizontally and trace upper right section. Refold vertically and trace left side of block to complete the design.

2. The stems must be stitched first, before appliquéing the center rose. Where required, appliqué the buds along with the stem as follows: (a) stitch up one side of stem; (b) stop at base of bud; (c) insert and stitch bud appliqué; (d) continue stitching stem where it is layered over bud; and (e) stitch down the other side of stem. The leaves can be added anytime after the stems are complete.

3. Appliqué the center rose in layers, beginning with the large outside rose and continuing to final layers. Before appliquéing the final layer, prepare flower center for reverse appliqué by placing flower center fabric between the two inside rose layers. Use reverse appliqué to appliqué final rose and then finish center. (See Reverse Appliqué instructions on pages 155–56.)

   Should you vary the foundation rose as suggested above, appliqué first rose layer and then follow directions given with rose version you have selected.

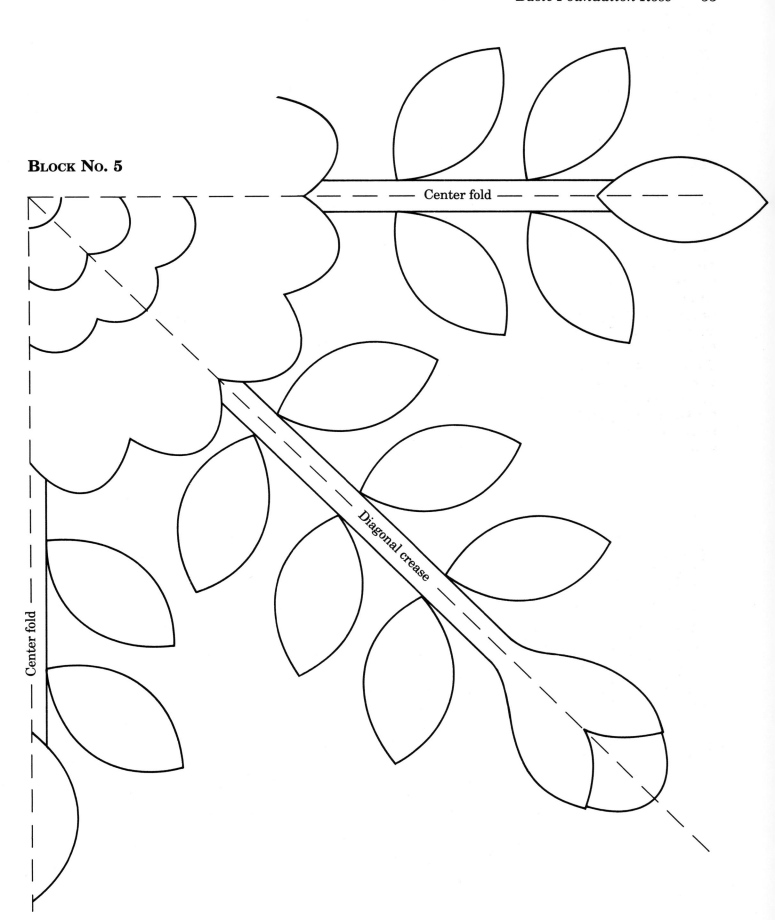

BLOCK NO. 5

Center fold

Center fold

Diagonal crease

BLOCK NO. 6
Foundation Rose with Berries

Finished Size: 16" x 16"

This foundation rose variation has more stems, leaves, and buds, making it more complex than the first version offered. The berries also make it more challenging, but the finished result is worth the extra effort.

CONSTRUCTION

1. Use the single pattern section on page 55 to make Master Pattern. First, trace the design onto the lower right section. Next, fold Master Pattern in half horizontally and trace upper right section. Refold vertically and trace left side of block to complete the design. Use the dot on center of each circle as a guide for placement of berries during appliqué; be sure to mark them on Master Pattern.

2. The stems must be stitched first, before appliquéing the center rose. Where required, appliqué the buds along with the stem as follows: (a) stitch up one side of stem; (b) stop at base of bud; (c) insert piece with outer bud petals (red on color photo) and stitch it down; (d) appliqué inside petal (yellow on color photo) to complete bud; (e) stitch down the other side of stem. The leaves can be added anytime after the stems are complete.

3. Add the berries after their stem is complete. Stitch them with the Perfect Circle Construction method described on pages 154–55. Begin with berry that covers tip of stem and then add remaining berries down either side of stem. Adjust placement of berries as necessary to evenly space them along stem.

4. Appliqué the center rose in layers, beginning with the largest outside rose. After completing each layer of the rose, cut away the overlapped previous layer to reduce bulk caused by several layers. Stitch the circles of flower center last.

BLOCK NO. 6

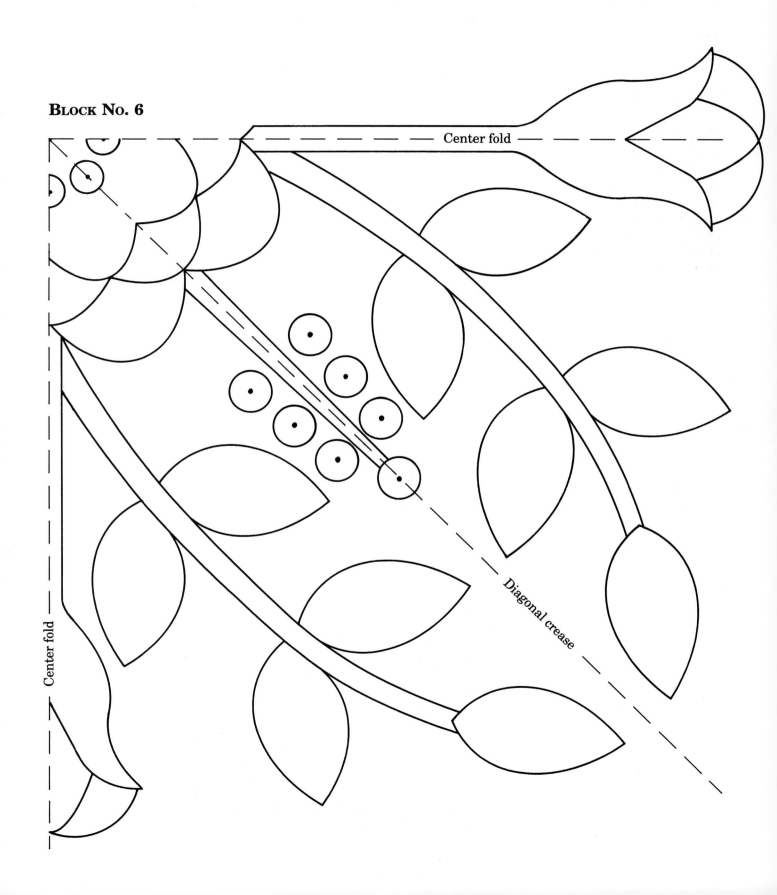

Center fold

Center fold

Diagonal crease

DIAGONAL STEM ROSE

This fourth category of rose design is one in which much variation is possible, and nineteenth-century quiltmakers did indeed produce many unusual and individualized arrangements in this category. Often, the only common element is the large diagonal stem that joins the design elements. My favorite design type from this category is the asymmetrical single rose and bud (Block No. 8, page 62). This seemingly awkward design becomes very elegant when multiple blocks are set together. Beth Crawford's quilt on page 135 features four of these asymmetrical blocks and a swag border, making an elegant wall quilt.

Occasionally, the diagonal stem–type design features a rose whose petals were pieced together. The pieced rose motif was then appliquéd into place. There are also a few examples of rose designs that are entirely pieced, including the joining of the floral motifs to the background fabric. Sketch 5 on page 57 is a late-nineteenth-century example of a completely pieced block.

DIAGONAL STEM ROSE SKETCHES

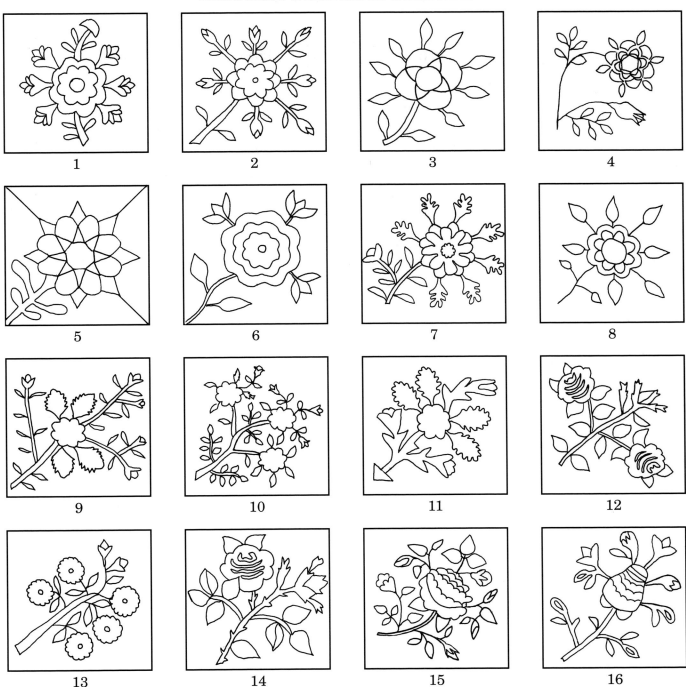

1. Carrie A. Hall and Rose G. Kretsinger, Romance of the American Patchwork Quilt, *p. 112; 2. Hall and Kretsinger,* Romance of the American Patchwork Quilt, *p. 114; 3. Carleton Safford and Robert Bishop,* America's Quilts and Coverlets, *p. 169; 4. Safford and Bishop,* America's Quilts and Coverlets, *p. 184; 5. Karoline Patterson Bresenhan and Nancy O'Bryant Puentes,* Lone Stars, *pp. 118–119; 6.* Lady's Circle Patchwork Quilts, *(Spring 1983), p. 26; 7. Robert Bishop,* New Discoveries in American Quilts, *p. 100; 8. Safford and Bishop,* America's Quilts and Coverlets, *p. 194; 9. Collection of DAR Museum, Acc. No. 80.33; 10.* 1984 Quilt Engagement Calendar, *Plate 9; 11. Jeannette Lasansky,* Pieced By Mother, *p. 67; 12. Marsha McDowell and Ruth D. Fitzgerald,* Michigan Quilts: 150 Years of a Textile Tradition, *p. 24; 13. Bresenhan and Puentes,* Lone Stars, *pp. 84–85; 14. Hall and Kretsinger,* Romance of the American Patchwork Quilt, *p. 170; 15. Bettina Havig,* Missouri Heritage Quilts, *p. 22; 16. Lasansky,* Pieced By Mother, *p. 56.*

BLOCK NO. 7
Rose with Stylized Tulips

Finished Size: 16" x 16"

Stitched by Kallie Dent, this whimsical plant arrangement of a rose and tulips on the same stalk is a good example of the hundreds of variations possible by combining elements from different sources. You should feel free to combine any elements you choose to make your own unique appliqué quilt. (See Design Ideas on page 148 for help in getting started.)

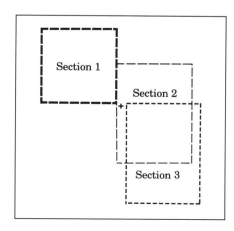

CONSTRUCTION

1. There are two pattern sections for this block. The main and secondary stem pattern section is found on page 61 and the two flowers on pages 59–60. Use the following steps to make Master Pattern:
   a. Using block section on page 61, trace the "skeleton" or base of design onto the lower right corner. Be sure to line up the diagonal crease and center fold indication marks.
   b. Trace half-rose motif on page 59 onto Master Pattern. (Trace only half of the rose; it will be completed in step d.) Again, be sure to line up diagonal crease and center fold indication marks before tracing.
   c. Using pattern on page 60, line up tulip on right stem and trace.
   d. Fold Master Pattern in half diagonally through the main stem and along half-rose you have drawn. When everything is lined up properly, trace other side of block to finish Master Pattern.
2. First appliqué secondary stems and then main stem. The leaves can be added anytime after the stems are complete.
3. Appliqué the rose in layers, beginning with outside rose and continuing to third layer. After appliqué of each rose layer is complete, cut away the previous layer where it is overlapped by motif just completed. (See instructions for Cutting Away Back

of Appliqué on page 154.) This will reduce bulk produced by several layers.

Before appliquéing the final rose layer, prepare flower center for reverse appliqué by placing flower center fabric between the rose layers. Use reverse appliqué to appliqué final rose and then finish flower center. (See instructions for Reverse Appliqué on pages 155–56.)

4. Appliqué the tulips in layers in the following order:
   a. First appliqué lower bulblike petals (pink on color photo). These petals should be cut as one large template that covers the entire bottom of the tulip.
   b. Appliqué tip of tulip (yellow on color photo). Make the template for tip of tulip as shown.
   c. Finish tulip with two red petals (as seen on color photo), one of which is reversed.

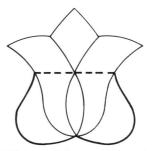

Cut lower petals as one large piece

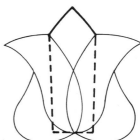

Template for tulip tip

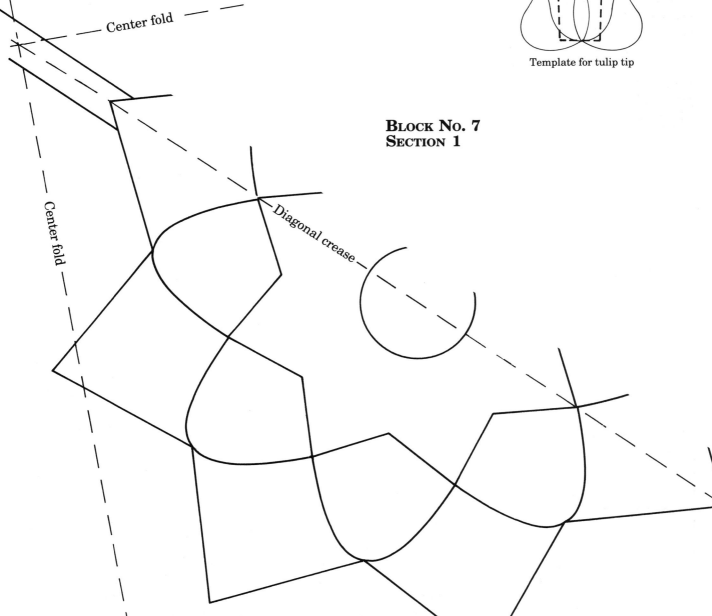

Center fold

Center fold

Diagonal crease

BLOCK NO. 7
SECTION 1

BLOCK NO. 7
SECTION 2

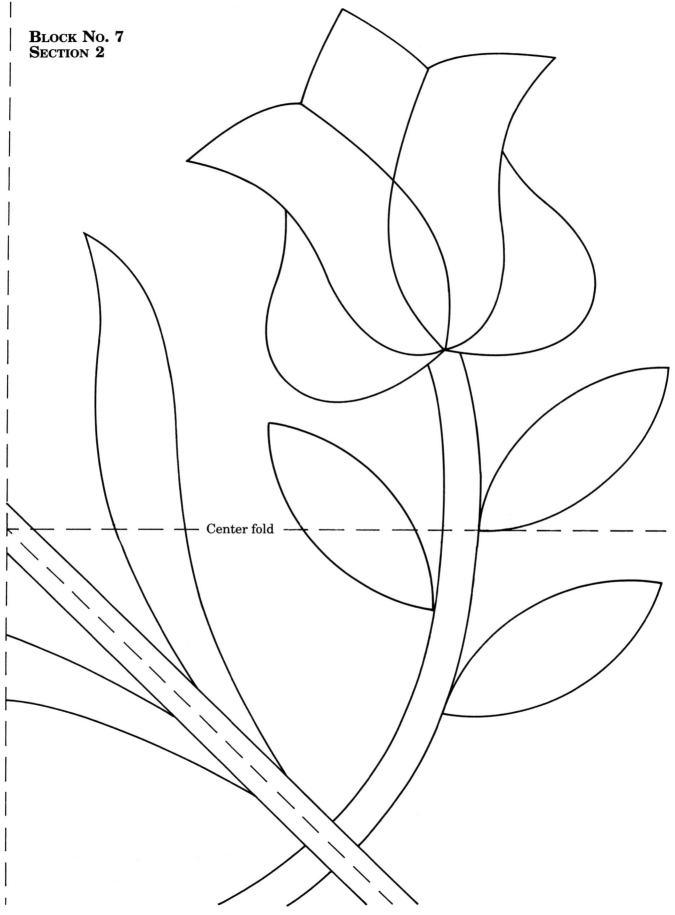

Center fold

BLOCK NO. 7
SECTION 3

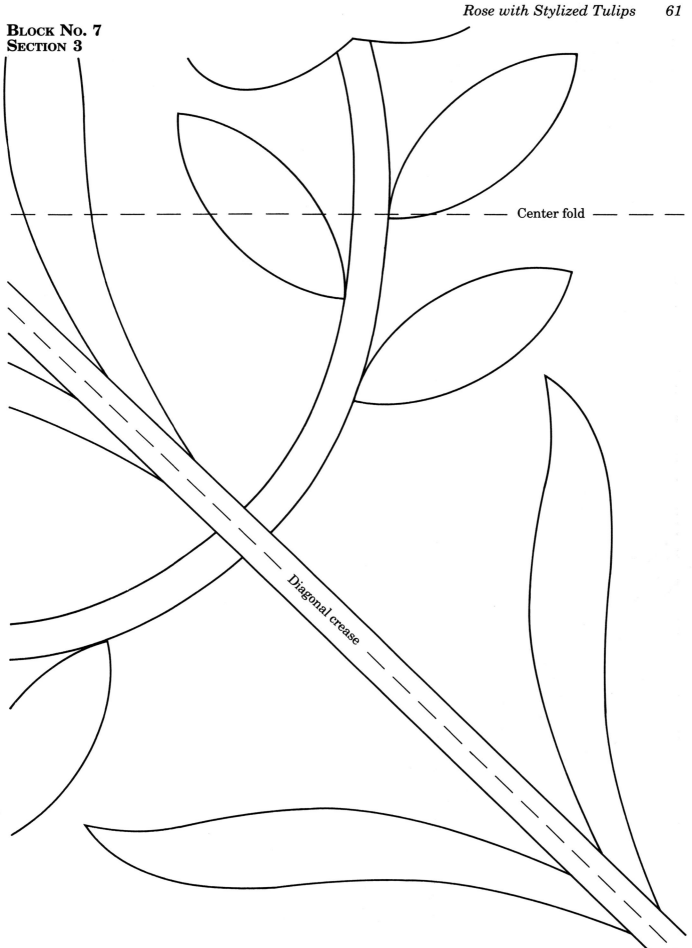

Center fold

Diagonal crease

BLOCK NO. 8
Asymmetrical Rose

Finished Size: 16" x 16"

This bold design was occasionally named "Pineapple" because of the unusual layering of the large rose motif. The version shown here, stitched by Charlotte Warr Andersen, and the one on page 135 are stitched in traditional rose colors, but the design would be equally effective in gold and rust, making it a Pineapple design.

CONSTRUCTION

1. The three sections to this pattern are located on pages 63–65. Trace the sections to make Master Pattern, beginning with the lower right corner of the block.
2. Stitch buds on secondary branches first, beginning with the outermost layer and working toward stem. Next, appliqué secondary stems.
3. Appliqué the large rose motif in layers, beginning with the outermost layer and stitching toward stem. The three green petal-shaped pieces at the top of the rose can be stitched anytime after the first rose layer. When the large rose is in place, stitch main stem and then large leaves on either side of center rose.

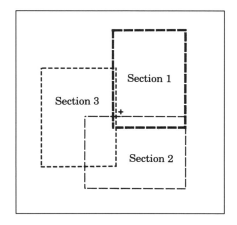

BLOCK NO. 8
SECTION 1

Center fold

Center fold

BLOCK NO. 8
SECTION 2

— — — Center fold — — — — — — — —

BLOCK NO. 8
SECTION 3

Center fold

Center fold

Other Flower Designs

Roses were universally used throughout the country on appliqué quilts; however, other different and unusual flower shapes were also found. This section will highlight a few of the other flower types.

The Tulip design had much universal appeal, which may have been due to the ease with which it could accurately be drawn and stitched. There are several sketched versions of the Tulip design presented on page 67, as well as full-size patterns on pages 70 and 72.

Another favorite design was the Prairie Flower or Rose Tree. Technically, this design fits into the rose category because of the main flower's shape, but it is included here because of the consistent use of its distinct design arrangement.

The bold and graphic cockscomb-type block is also presented in this section. Since many examples of this distinctive design are found in Pennsylvania, it may have originated there.

In addition, there are unusual appliqué designs found in regional areas of the country. Included in this section is one such design titled "Cotton Boll" (pattern on page 89).

Also presented are a few other seldom-used appliqué designs.

TULIP

Nineteenth-century women chose tulips as their second most frequently stitched red-and-green appliqué flower subject. Perhaps it was the simple, yet realistic, lines of the tulip that appealed to them, or maybe it was the symbolism of the tulip that made it so popular. Tulips suggest springtime and all the cheerful, bright days that come with spring. I designed and appliquéd my quilt, "Bride of Tulip Valley" (page 125), one February, in an effort to bring a little spring into a long, cold winter. Other quiltmakers may have been inspired in the same way. Tulips and springtime bring to mind new beginnings, thus making tulips a logical choice for the subject of a nineteenth-century bridal quilt.

Tulips were a popular appliqué motif again during the 1930s, when interest in quiltmaking revived for a time. Pastel colors were the favorite choice during that time, and Tulip quilts of that era had a different, but appealing, look.

Tulip appliqué falls into three distinct design arrangements:

The crossed-stem type (Sketches 1–7) is a symmetrical and formal arrangement. As you can see from the sketched versions, the crossed-stem tulips can be depicted simply or carefully detailed, with equal success. "Bride of Tulip Valley" fits into this category as a formal arrangement that includes two other appliqué blocks (patterns on pages 71–76).

A more spontaneous approach is the use of a diagonal main stem (Sketches 8–14) as the pattern format. Many charming variations are found in this popular category. The diagonal stem–type tulip usually features three tulips as its main focus. Occasionally, a quiltmaker would add other elements to enhance her

TULIP SKETCHES

1. *Marsha MacDowell and Ruth D. Fitzgerald,* Michigan Quilts, 150 Years of a Textile Tradition, *p. 53; 2. Marguerite Ickis,* The Standard Book of Quiltmaking and Collecting, *p. 102; 3. Ickis,* The Standard Book of Quiltmaking and Collecting, *p. 109; 4. Thomas K. Woodard and Blanche Greenstein,* Crib Quilts and Other Small Wonders, *p. 51; 5. Ruth E. Finley,* Old Patchwork Quilts and the Women Who Made Them, *Plate 58; 6. Carleton Safford and Robert Bishop,* America's Quilts and Coverlets, *p. 192; 7. 1986 Quilt Engagement Calendar, Plate 5; 8. Bets Ramsey and Merikay Waldvogel,* The Quilts of Tennessee: Images of Domestic Life Prior to 1930, *p. xvi; 9. Finley,* Old Patchwork Quilts and the Women Who Made Them, *Plate 37; 10. 1984 Quilt Engagement Calendar, Plate 55; 11. Carrie A. Hall and Rose G. Kretsinger,* Romance of the American Patchwork Quilt, *p. 122; 12. Safford and Bishop,* America's Quilts and Coverlets, *p. 187; 13. Hall and Kretsinger,* Romance of the American Patchwork Quilt, *p. 122; 14. Bettina Havig,* Missouri Heritage Quilts, *pp. 16–17; 15. McDowell and Fitzgerald,* Michigan Quilts, *p. 54; 16. Ickis,* The Standard Book of Quiltmaking and Collecting, *p. 49.*

design, such as the bird perched on a branch in Sketch 10.

A more organized version of the diagonal stem–type is the Tulip quilt shown on page 131. Margaret Jane McMath followed a formal layout for her quilt blocks but individualized her quilt by quilting a hand print (maybe hers) in each of the four corners of the border.

A less common version is the single Tulip block (Sketches 15 and 16). This simple and direct approach requires more blocks for a quilt but allows much variation in quilt settings.

BLOCK No. 9
Tulip Basket

Finished Size: 16" x 16"

Springtime can be preserved forever when you make this four-basket arrangement of tulips, stitched by Maureen Blosch. With this pattern, Kristine Haas expanded on the basket theme in her quilt by adding a Tiny Basket pieced border (page 135). Kristine's quilt is an excellent example of how just one block can be used to make a charming baby or wall quilt.

CONSTRUCTION

1. Use the single pattern section on page 70 to make Master Pattern. First, trace the design onto the lower right section. Next, fold Master Pattern in half horizontally and trace upper right section. Refold vertically and trace left side of block to complete the design.

2. Stitch the stems first and then the basket. The teardrop detail on the baskets is optional; it is stitched in reverse appliqué techniques. (See Reverse Appliqué instructions on pages 155–56.)

3. Add the tulips next. Stitch the center tulip's outside layer (red on color photo) first and then the lower body section. Stitch the two outside tulips' center sections (yellow on color photo), then the outside petals. It is not necessary to appliqué areas of a motif that will be covered by another appliqué piece. For example, each center section of the outside tulips is appliquéd only a stitch or two beyond the place where the outside petal will cover it.

4. Add the leaves last and adjust as necessary to keep them from overlapping onto flowers or basket.

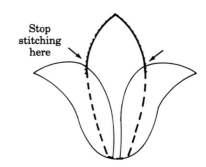

Stop stitching here

BLOCK NO. 9

Center fold

Center fold

Diagonal crease

BLOCK NO. 10
Hearts and Tulips

Finished Size: 12" x 12"

Blocks No. 10, No. 11, and No. 12 are all used in the "Bride of Tulip Valley" quilt (see pages 125–26 for detailed instructions on preparing blocks and constructing quilt).

CONSTRUCTION

1. Make a 12" square Master Pattern by tracing the single pattern section on page 72. First, trace the design onto the lower right section. Next, fold Master Pattern in half horizontally and trace upper right section. Refold vertically and trace left side of block to complete the design.
2. Cut background fabric 14" square (this allows block to be cut down to 12½" after appliqué is complete).
3. Appliqué center rose first, then appliqué stems. Add hearts, tulips, and leaves in order, as shown.

BLOCK NO. 10

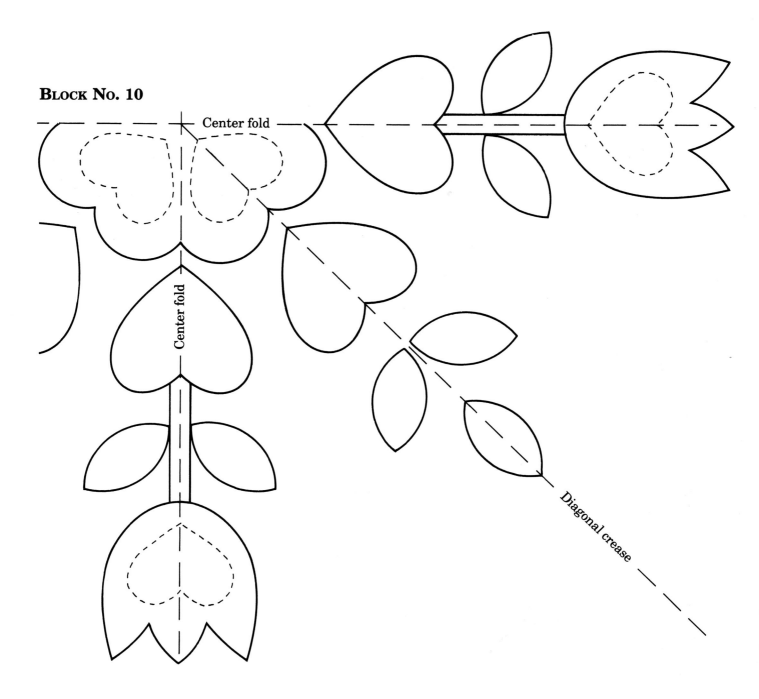

Center fold

Center fold

Diagonal crease

– – – – – – – Dotted line indicates quilting

BLOCK NO. 11
Crossed Branches

Finished Size: 12" x 12"

Blocks No. 10, No. 11, and No. 12 are all used in the "Bride of Tulip Valley" quilt (see pages 125–26 for detailed instructions on preparing blocks and constructing quilt).

CONSTRUCTION

1. Make a 12" square Master Pattern by tracing the pattern on page 74, which is one-half of the complete pattern. On the top where the tip of the heart is cut off, retrace it from lower heart. Fold Master Pattern vertically along center line and trace other half to complete design.
2. Appliqué the stems. Make bias strip that is ⅜" wide (finished width) and 22" long for each block. (See Bias-Strip Construction on page 155.) Cut bias strip in half so you have two 11" lengths and appliqué each half as a stem.
3. Appliqué hearts and leaves.

BLOCK NO. 11

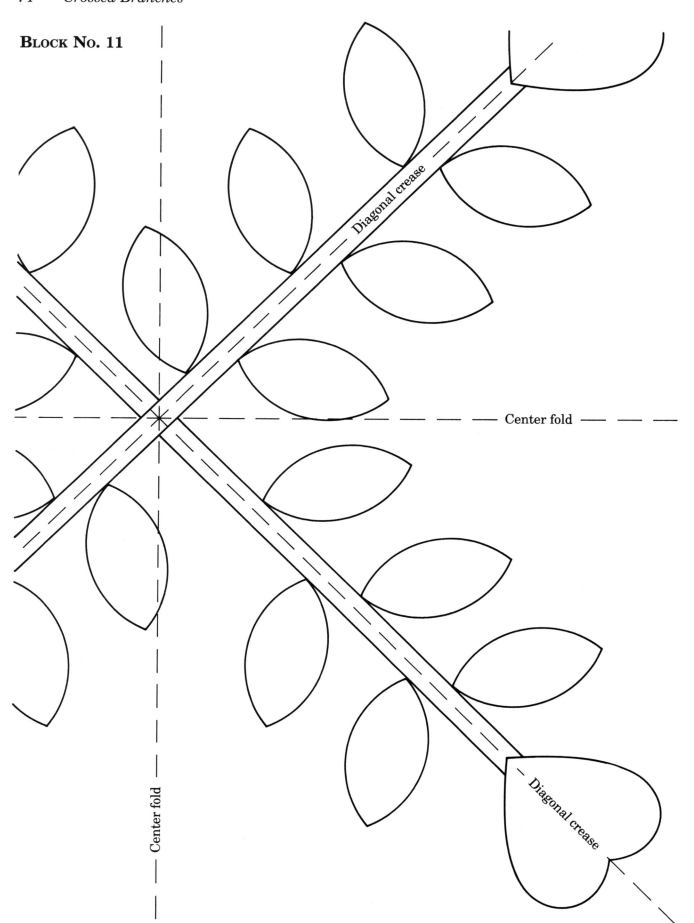

BLOCK NO. 12
Heart Wreath

Finished Size: 12" x 12"

Blocks No. 10, No. 11, and No. 12 are all used in the "Bride of Tulip Valley" quilt (see pages 125–26 for detailed instructions on preparing blocks and constructing quilt).

CONSTRUCTION

1. Make a 12" square Master Pattern by tracing the pattern on page 76, which is one-half of the complete pattern. Where the tips of leaves have been cut off, use another complete leaf on the wreath to draw remainder of leaf. Fold Master Pattern in half vertically and trace opposite side of wreath and center heart.

2. The following is an easy way to appliqué the vine in the center of the Heart Wreath block:

   a. Photocopy heart-shaped vine of Master Pattern.

   b. Cut around only the outside of vine on photocopy. Trace this large pattern onto your vine fabric. Cut out and appliqué the large heart (inside of heart vine will be cut away later). By appliquéing this large piece, the vine is stabilized while stitching for a smooth, clean appliqué line.

   c. Cut vine off from paper pattern and discard vine, leaving smaller inside heart shape.

   d. Place this smaller paper heart on large appliquéd fabric heart. Trace around small paper heart pattern. This marks the inside stitching line of heart vine.

   e. Trim to ³/₁₆" beyond pencil line and finish appliqué of vine. The large piece of fabric that is trimmed away from the inside of the heart vine can be used to cut out other leaves for the vine.

3. Add leaves and center heart.

BLOCK NO. 12

Center fold

Center fold

– – – – – – Dotted line indicates quilting

COCKSCOMB

The Cockscomb design is depicted in three distinct styles that have similar characteristics. All of the designs in this category were consistently named "Cockscomb" or "Coxcomb." One other Cockscomb-type block combines "currants" with a different Cockscomb motif, and that design type is shown in the Fruits and Nuts section on page 98.

Many of the Cockscomb quilts that I cataloged were documented as having been made in Pennsylvania, leading to the possibility that the designs may have originated there. Also, the bold flowers and graphic arrangements are typical of Pennsylvania-German designs, which is further evidence of a Pennsylvania origin.

The sixteen sketches on page 78 illustrate the three types of Cockscomb designs. Sketches 1–4 show pot- or basket-type containers with the cockscomb flowers arranged in them. Sketches 5–7 are asymmetrical Cockscomb designs that feature two flowers and one large leaf. "Thistle" is another name occasionally assigned to this design arrangement. There is an unusual 1850s "Thistle" quilt found on page 142. This quilt was constructed as two separate pieces. One part was made as a bed covering, and the other was made as a pillow covering.

The remaining sketches are crossed design–type blocks. Sketches 13–16 are cut out in a way similar to scherenschnitte (German paper cutting). Many of the crossed-design examples shown in the sketches are attributed to a Pennsylvania origin.

COCKSCOMB SKETCHES

1. *Ruth E. Finley,* Old Patchwork Quilts and the Women Who Made Them, *Plate 70; 2. Robert Bishop,* New Discoveries in American Quilts, *p. 75; 3. 1982 Quilt Engagement Calendar, Plate 32; 4. Carrie A. Hall and Rose G. Kretsinger,* The Romance of the Patchwork Quilt in America, *p. 120; 5. Bishop,* New Discoveries in American Quilts, *p. 75; 6. 1988 Quilt Engagement Calendar, Plate 25; 7. private collection; 8. Jonathan Holstein and John Finley,* Kentucky Quilts 1800–1900, *p. 34; 9. 1987 Quilt Engagement Calendar, Plate 55; 10.* Lady's Circle Patchwork Quilts *(Summer 1982), p. 11; 11. Thomas K. Woodard and Blanche Greenstein,* Crib Quilts and Other Small Wonders, *p. 53; 12. Jeannette Lasansky,* In the Heart of Pennsylvania, *p. 39; 13. Marguerite Ickis,* The Standard Book of Quiltmaking and Collecting, *p. 72; 14. Lasansky,* In the Heart of Pennsylvania, *p. 44; 15. 1984 Quilt Engagement Calander, Plate 46; 16. Lasansky,* In the Heart of Pennsylvania, *p. 39.*

BLOCK NO. 13
Cockscomb in Basket with Birds

Finished Size: 16" x 16"

The strong graphic design of the cockscomb flower, combined with the curious birds, make this block hard to resist. Kristine Haas stitched four of these blocks and set them together with bold flying-geese sashing. Her outside appliqué border complements and echoes the Cockscomb design. Kristine's quilt is shown on page 139.

CONSTRUCTION

1. Trace the two pattern sections (bottom and top), found on pages 80 and 81, onto one-half of Master Pattern. Fold Master Pattern in half vertically and use a light box or window to trace the mirror image of the design onto other side.
2. Stitch the secondary stems first; stitch the main stem through the center of the arrangement after the secondary stems are complete.
3. The cockscomb flower is made up of just two pattern pieces found on page 81. To stitch this flower, first place a large piece of accent fabric (yellow in color photo) as indicated in illustration. You do not need to turn under the edges of this accent piece since all edges are covered by the appliqué of the two pattern pieces. Add the green flower base next; this piece will cover raw edges on bottom of accent fabric. Finally, appliqué top, or blossom, of cockscomb. This final appliqué piece will finish covering the accent fabric as the sawtoothlike portions are stitched into place. To give the flower the illusion of piecing, make sure the sawtooth points touch the green base piece.
4. Appliqué the birds in the following order: (a) beak; (b) bird body; and (c) wing. Embroider the feet in stem stitch.
5. Appliqué the berries, leaves, and basket. Basket is in two pieces: appliqué the base first and the upper trim last.

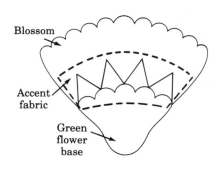

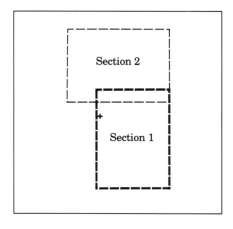

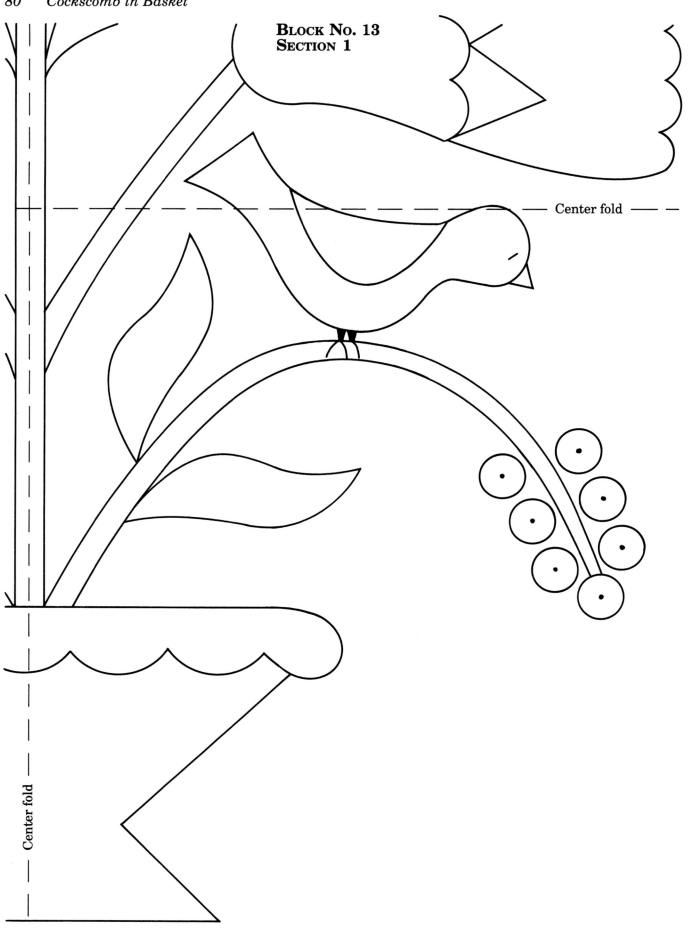

BLOCK NO. 13
SECTION 1

Center fold

Center fold

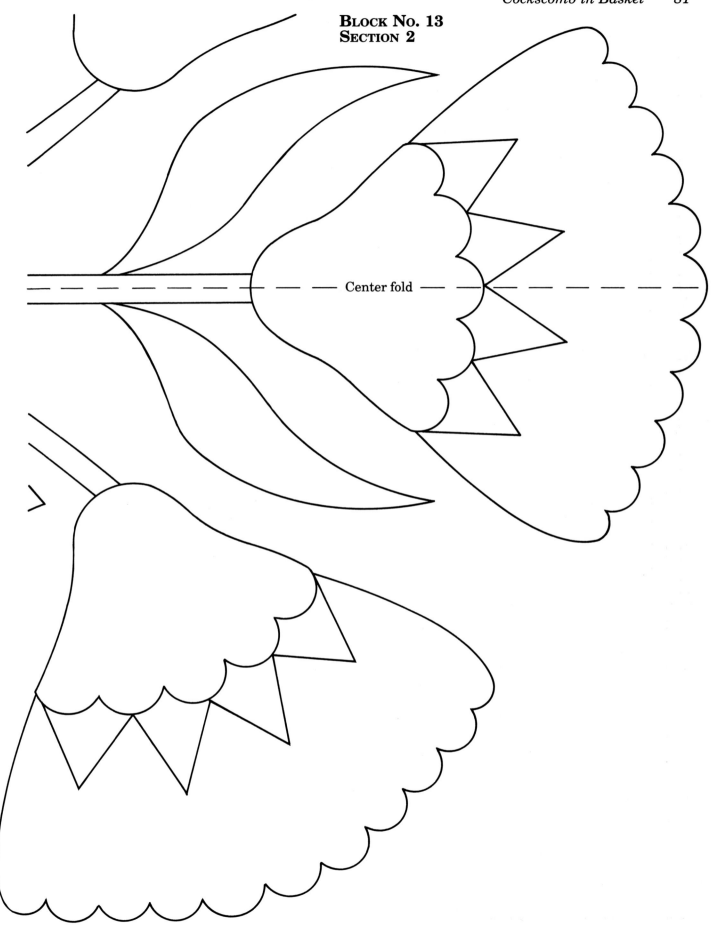

**BLOCK NO. 13
SECTION 2**

Center fold

PRAIRIE FLOWER AND OTHERS

The distinct open wreath with a single rose and triple buds arrangement, commonly called "Prairie Flower," was a popular pattern during the nineteenth century. It was revived during the 1930s when it was published in at least two quilt resource books of the time. During both eras, the basic format of this design remained the same; however, the same main rose and/or triple buds were rarely repeated on any of the many examples found. Other names given this design include "Rose Tree," "Rambling Rose," and "Missouri Rose." The eight versions of the Prairie Flower shown in Sketches 1–8 illustrate the differences and similarities of this popular design.

Sketches 9–11 are quilt designs frequently called "Meadow Daisy" or "Mexican Rose." The full-size pattern given in Block No. 16 (page 89) is a design called "Cotton Boll," which could easily have been adapted from the Meadow Daisy format. During my research, I located photos of three quilts of the Cotton Boll design. All of the quilts were from southern states. The design format remained the same on all the quilts, but there were slight variations in fabric color arrangement on the quilts.[27] Sketches 12 and 13 are of a unique design with various names, including "Ladies' Dream," "Chestnut Bud," and "Mrs. Harris' Colonial Rose." During the 1930s, the version in Sketch 13 was sold through a mail-order pattern business.

Shown in Sketches 14 and 15 are two "Laurel Leaves" block variations. This block was seldom used for a whole quilt; it was much more frequently incorporated into album quilts. A 12" pattern, titled "Crossed Branches," is another version of this block and can be seen on page 73.

Sketch 16 is of a seemingly original flower shape combined with tulips. However, an almost identical flower pattern is given in this book as Block No. 17 on page 91 and is a reproduction of an 1820s quilt made in Virginia. Both quilts were given the name "Rose of Sharon" when photos of them were published. It is interesting to compare how two quiltmakers using the same unusual flower stitched such dissimilar arrangements.

PRAIRIE FLOWER AND OTHER SKETCHES

1   2   3   4

5   6   7   8

9   10   11   12

13   14   15   16

1. Carrie A. Hall and Rose G. Kretsinger, The Romance of the Patchwork Quilt in America, *p. 146; 2. Barbara Brackman,* American Patchwork Quilt, *Plate 47; 3. Jonathan Holstein and John Finley,* Kentucky Quilts 1800–1900, *p. 24; 4. Karoline Patterson Bresenhan and Nancy O'Bryant Puentes,* Lone Stars: A Legacy of Texas Quilts, 1836–1936, *p. 41; 5. Bresenhan and Puentes,* Lone Stars, *p. 49; 6.* Lady's Circle Patchwork Quilts *(Fall 1982), p. 28; 7.* Lady's Circle Patchwork Quilts *(February/March 1987), p. 22; 8. Marguerite Ickis,* The Standard Book of Quiltmaking and Collecting, *p. 113; 9. Hall and Kretsinger,* The Romance of the Patchwork Quilt in America, *p. 104; 10.* Lady's Circle Patchwork Quilts, *No. 20 (1980), p. 16; 11. Bresenhan and Puentes,* Lone Stars, *pp. 104–105; 12. Bets Ramsey and Merikay Waldvogel,* The Quilts of Tennessee: Images of Domestic Life Prior to 1930, *pp. 58–59; 13. Brackman,* American Patchwork Quilt, *Plate 35; 14. Carleton Safford and Robert Bishop,* America's Quilts and Coverlets, *p. 158; 15. Edwin Binney III and Gail Binney-Winslow,* Homage to Amanda: Two Hundred Years of American Quilts, *p. 49; 16. Ruth E. Finley,* Old Patchwork Quilts and the Women Who Made Them, *Plate 66.*

BLOCK NO. 14
Prairie Flower

Finished Size: 16" x 16"

This versatile pattern can be arranged on your background fabric "straight on," as shown here, or placed "on point," as shown on Minerva Colemere's quilt on page 138. Either option is equally lovely. To set off Minerva's four Prairie Flower blocks, I designed a wreath block that uses the same flower and leaves she used for the center of her quilt. The Prairie Flower Wreath is given as Block No. 15 on page 87. The same component parts are repeated in the border of Minerva's quilt.

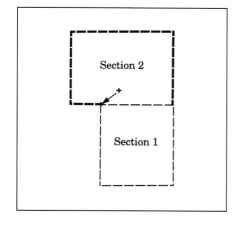

CONSTRUCTION

1. Use the two pattern sections for this block on pages 85–86 to make Master Pattern. First, trace the bottom section onto Master Pattern. Next, line up and trace the upper pattern section. The tip of the side bud can be traced from the bud given in the upper pattern section for this block. Fold Master Pattern in half vertically to trace left side of wreath. Should you decide to place this pattern "on point," make Master Pattern as described above and then retrace it onto another 16" square of paper that has been rotated a half-turn.

2. In the version of this block that Minerva Colemere stitched, she added an extra yellow layer at the base of each bud. You may choose to add this extra piece to your quilt, depending on the fabrics you use.

3. Begin stitching by attaching the half-circle vine. Make the vine from a 20" x ³/₈" (finished width) bias. (See Bias-Strip Construction on page 155.) Use leftover bias piece (approximately 3" long) for stem at the top center of block.

4. Add buds and leaves after stems are complete. Appliqué buds in the following order: (a) largest outside bud piece (red on color photo); (b) inside bud piece (yellow); (c) base of bud (green); and (d) detail at top of bud (green).

5. Add large center rose. Appliqué large outside layer first and continue to third layer. After appliqué of each layer is com-

plete, cut away the previous layer where it is overlapped by
motif just completed. This will reduce the bulk produced by
several layers. (See instructions for Cutting Away Back of
Appliqué on page 154.)

6. Before appliquéing the final rose layer, prepare flower center
for reverse appliqué by placing flower center fabric between
the rose layers. Use reverse appliqué to appliqué final rose and
then finish flower center. (See Reverse Appliqué instructions
on pages 155–56.)

**BLOCK NO. 14
SECTION 1**

Center fold

Center fold

BLOCK NO. 14
SECTION 2

Center fold

Center fold

BLOCK NO. 15
Prairie Flower Wreath

Finished Size: 16" x 16"

This wreath complements the Prairie Flower block (Block No. 14, page 84) and can be used as an alternating design in conjunction with the traditional Prairie Flower. Minerva Colemere used this block for the center of her Prairie Flower quilt (see page 138).

CONSTRUCTION

1. Use the single pattern section for this block on page 88 to make Master Pattern. First, trace the bottom right section. Next, fold Master Pattern in half horizontally and trace upper right section of block. Refold Master Pattern in half vertically and trace left side of design to complete pattern.
2. The center vine can be constructed by either of the following methods:
   a. Use instructions given for Heart Wreath in Block No. 12 (page 75). This method is preferred since there are no bias ends to join.
   b. Make a 33" x ³⁄₈" (finished width) bias. Appliqué to background fabric and join ends.
3. Appliqué buds and leaves around outside of vine. Stitch the buds in two layers, beginning with larger outside layer.
4. The large center rose is the same one that is used on the Prairie Flower, Block No. 14. (See step 5 on pages 84–85 for appliqué instructions.)
5. Appliqué the leaves surrounding center rose between each rose scallop. You may need to make slight adjustments while stitching inside leaf points to ensure that leaves do not overlap onto rose petals.

BLOCK NO. 15

BLOCK NO. 16
Cotton Boll

Finished Size: 16" x 16"

The graphic, bold arrangement of this block makes it easy to identify. The North Carolina Quilt Project documented four quilts that use this design. All of the quilts they identified were made around 1860. The Cotton Boll quilt seen in *Arkansas Quilts* was appliquéd shortly before the turn of the century, making it a later version than the North Carolina quilts, but the design was unaltered on any of the quilts. "Chrysanthemum" is another name used to identify this design.

CONSTRUCTION

1. Use the single pattern section for this block on page 90 to make Master Pattern. First, trace the design onto the lower right corner. Next, fold Master Pattern in half horizontally and trace upper right corner. Then, fold Master Pattern in half vertically and trace left side of block.

2. Make a template of the entire stem, including bud base on stem ends. Begin appliqué with the two stems.

3. When the stems are complete, begin adding the flower petals. Five petal templates are required to stitch the Cotton Boll blossom. Reverse the templates for the alternate side of flower. It is best to number the templates with corresponding numbers marked on Master Pattern to avoid confusion, since the petal shapes are all similar. Start appliqué with center petal and add petals down either side of bud base. To ensure that points of petals touch base, begin stitching petal about ½" from point that touches base. Appliqué down to point and then around point and rest of petal. This way, if the piece shifts slightly during appliqué, it will not affect the spacing of the flower petals.

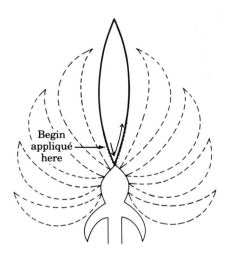

Begin appliqué here

BLOCK No. 16

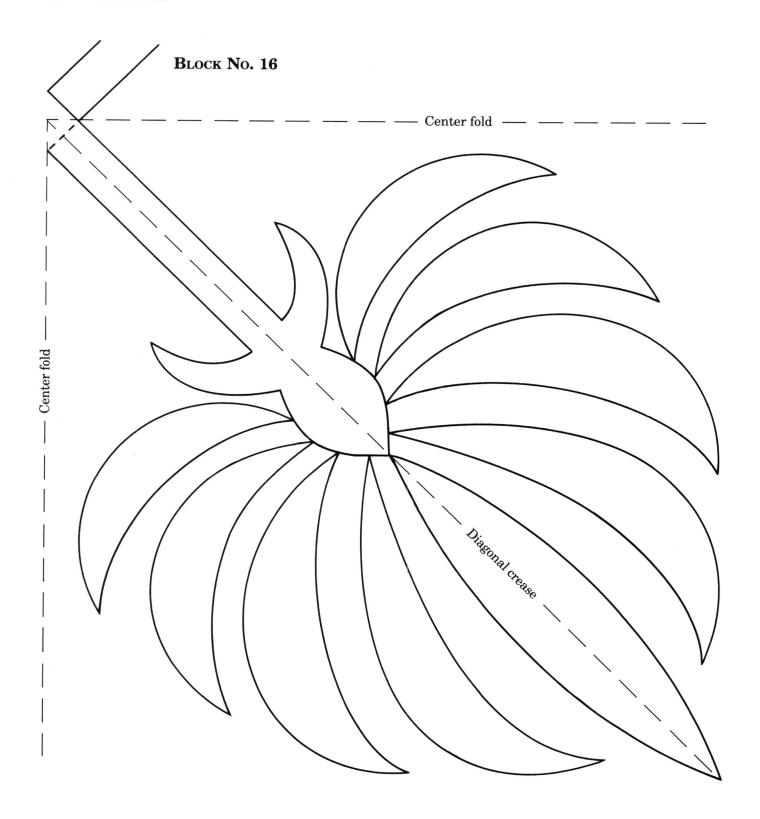

Center fold

Center fold

Diagonal crease

BLOCK NO. 17
Cactus Blossom

Finished Size: 16" x 16"

Even though this flower shape was used in two quilts called "Rose of Sharon," the design is renamed here to describe my interpretation of the distinct flower both quilts share. The block shown here is a reproduction of the block used on a quilt made in Virginia in 1820 by Charlotte Pankey. Charlotte's quilt has been preserved in perfect condition by each generation, in spite of difficult times, as a family symbol that cannot be bought or sold at any price.

CONSTRUCTION

1. Use the single pattern section for this block on page 92 to make Master Pattern. First, trace the bottom right section. Next, fold Master Pattern horizontally and trace upper right section of block. Then, fold Master Pattern in half vertically and trace left side of design.
2. Appliqué center scalloped ring.
3. Add the stem section as one large continuous piece.
4. Add cactus flowers. There are four pattern pieces. The outside red piece is cut large enough to fill in background of blossom. All other pieces are cut out in size shown. Appliqué flower in the following order: (a) outside petal pieces (red on color photo); (b) half-circle piece (pink); (c) leaf base (green); and (d) flower center (yellow). You may need to make adjustments when stitching the green leaf base and yellow flower center to ensure the flower center fits without touching the upper half-circle piece.
5. Appliqué leaves after flowers are in place.

Red

BLOCK NO. 17

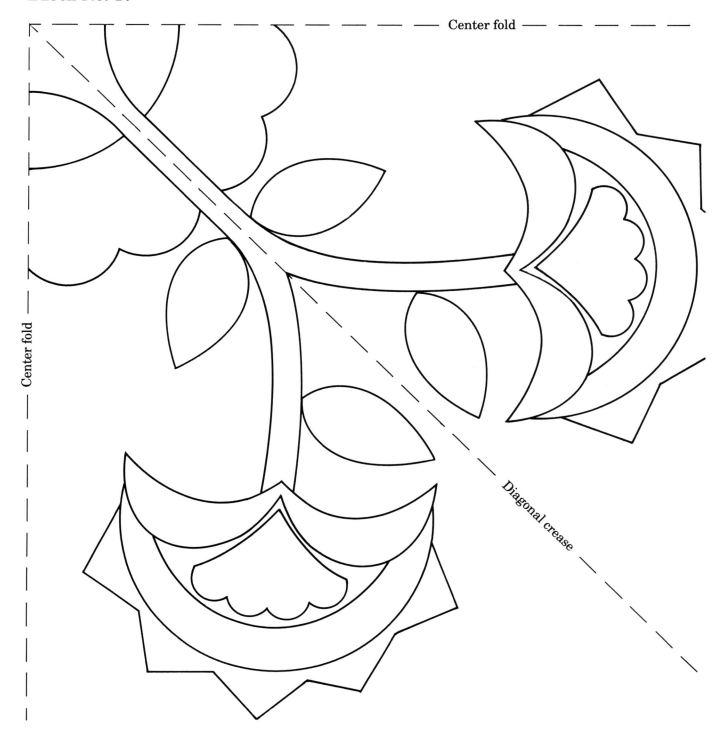

Center fold

Center fold

Diagonal crease

Fruits and Nuts

While cataloging red-and-green appliqué quilts, I found a definite category that depicted fruits and nuts. Some of the familiar patterns in this category are Oak Leaf and Reel, Pineapple, Pomegranate or Love Apple, and Cherry Wreath.

The term "nuts" is used loosely here and actually only represents the oak leaf and its fruit, the acorn. However, there are many oak-leaf variations, and the sixteen sketched versions on page 110 illustrate just a few of them. Also included is a full-size Oak Leaf pattern on pages 111–12.

It is interesting that nineteenth-century quiltmakers chose to depict some fruits on their red-and-green appliqué quilts, but rarely vegetables. The appliquéd fruits they used, including pineapples, pomegranates, strawberries, and cherries, were exotic by nineteenth-century standards. Perhaps it was because vegetables were considered a diet staple, and therefore ordinary, that they were not so honored.

In comparison, fruits today are seldom depicted in appliqué. Instead, flowers are a common subject. Using the same criteria of the ordinary versus luxury in today's world, fruits are as plentiful and easily available as vegetables, and we view them as staples. However, a gift of flowers is still unexpected and considered a luxury. Can it be that we, as quiltmakers did one hundred years ago, stitch into our best quilts the things that we value as a special part of our lives?

The following patterns and sketches include a berries-type category, a pineapple-pomegranate category, and an oak-leaf category.

BERRIES

Many berries are depicted on appliqué quilts. Since they were nearly all stitched in red, it is difficult to decide if the appliquéd berries are meant to be cherries, grapes, currants, or any of a number of other varieties. Ruth Finley discussed this question in her book, *Old Patchwork Quilts and the Women Who Made Them*:

> The little round patches showing in the border are red and precisely the size of the early sour cherries of the famous pies of our grandmothers. But they are bunched like grapes and are attached to a vine; so they can hardly have been meant for cherries. Just what they were intended to represent would be hard to say, yet their effect is exceedingly delightful.[28]

Occasionally, the name given to the quilt indicates the proper fruit, such as the Poke Stalk quilt (page 19) made by Elizabeth Currier Foster; its name and history definitely identify the berries. Also, the Cockscomb and Currants design is universally titled so there is no mistaking what kind of berries are depicted. However, many others are not so easily identified, especially when they are

BERRY SKETCHES

1   2   3   4

5   6   7   8

9   10   11   12

13   14   15   16

1. Marsha MacDowell and Ruth D. Fitzgerald, Michigan Quilts: 150 Years of a Textile Tradition, *p. 64; 2. Carrie A. Hall and Rose G. Kretsinger,* The Romance of the Patchwork Quilt in America, *p. 106; 3. 1982* Quilt Engagement Calendar, *Plate 3; 4. Marsha McCloskey,* Christmas Quilts, *p. 25; 5. MacDowell and Fitzgerald,* Michigan Quilts, *p. 64; 6. Jeannette Lasansky,* In the Heart of Pennsylvania, *p. 43; 7. Sandi Fox,* Small Endearments, *Plate 43; 8. Lasansky,* In the Heart of Pennsylvania, *p. 42; 9. Thomas K. Woodard and Blanche Greenstein,* Crib Quilts and Other Small Wonders, *p. 45; 10. Cyril I. Nelson and Carter Houck,* Quilt Engagement Calendar Treasury, *p. 138; 11. Bettina Havig,* Missouri Heritage Quilts, *pp. 66–67; 12. Nelson and Houck,* Quilt Engagement Calendar Treasury, *p. 12; 13. Lady's Circle Patchwork Quilts, (Fall 1982), p. 30; 14. Jonathan Holstein and John Finley,* Kentucky Quilts 1800–1900, *pp. 38–39; 15. Lasansky,* In the Heart of Pennsylvania, *p. 35; 16. Bets Ramsey and Merikay Waldvogel,* The Quilts of Tennessee: Images of Domestic Life Prior to 1930, *p. 46.*

used as an accent design element with other flowers. The sketches shown here are categorized according to design elements and are generally identified with a name.

Sketches 1–8 are likely candidates for the "cherry" name because of the leaves used with them. Sketch 9 is probably a grape wreath, again because of the leaf used with the fruit, and the quilt block in Sketch 10 was taken from a quilt titled "Cherry Tree," thus identifying its fruit.

Sketches 11–16 are all variations of the universally named Cockscomb and Currants block. Another name occasionally assigned to this design format is "Poinsettia."

BLOCK NO. 18
Strawberry Wreath

Finished Size: 16" x 16"

Since round berries have been included in many other patterns in this book, I used strawberries in this wreath arrangement instead of the traditional cherry motif. Strawberry wreaths were frequently included in nineteenth-century album quilts, but when a quiltmaker decided to make a whole quilt using strawberries as her main subject, she usually used a cluster arrangement instead of a wreath. Sketches 15 and 16 on page 114 show unusual and original strawberry designs. The pattern presented here is one of the most difficult patterns in this book and is not recommended as your first block.

CONSTRUCTION

1. Use the single pattern section on page 97 to make Master Pattern. First, trace the design onto the lower right section. Next, fold Master Pattern in half horizontally and trace upper right section. Refold vertically and trace left side of block, completing wreath.
2. Stitch the two secondary stems on each quarter section of this wreath first, before the center vine. Be sure to allow plenty of seam allowance where secondary stems are overlapped by center vine.
3. Appliqué the center vine. I recommend that you use the construction method described in Block No. 12, step 2 on page 75. This method is preferred since there are no bias ends to join.
4. Add remaining leaves, blossoms, and berries to block, referring often to Master Pattern for overlapped leaves and blossoms.
5. Embroidery detail on strawberries was stitched with one strand of yellow embroidery floss using the straight stitch–embroidery technique.

BLOCK NO. 18

BLOCK NO. 19
Cockscomb and Currants

Finished Size: 16" x 16"

While studying the different variations of this block for ideas in designing this version, I noticed that the center flower looked like a poinsettia (some of them were, in fact, named "Poinsettia"). I also noticed that the cockscomb piece resembled an angel with outspread wings. So, I drew this version to resemble an angel even more, including a halo for her head. Several of these blocks stitched in pastels to define the angel and the rest of the motifs in Christmas red and green would make a striking Christmas quilt.

CONSTRUCTION

1. Use the single pattern section on page 99 to make Master Pattern. First, trace the design onto the lower right section. Next, trace the pattern onto the upper right section; continue tracing the pattern in a counterclockwise direction around the Master Pattern. Use dot on center of each circle as a guide for placement of berries during appliqué; be sure to mark them on Master Pattern.

2. Begin stitching with the four stems that berries are arranged along. Add the center circle of poinsettia flower next. Carefully position the flower petals to make sure the appropriate petal is aligned with corner of block. The cockscomb or "angel" should line up properly with corner. Appliqué.

3. Add the cockscomb or "angel." The reverse appliqué detail on this piece is optional. (See Reverse Appliqué instructions on pages 155–56.)

4. Appliqué the "head and halo of angel," or cockscomb bud. Then, add berries along stem, beginning with berry that covers tip of stem. Appliqué remaining berries down either side of stem.

BLOCK NO. 19

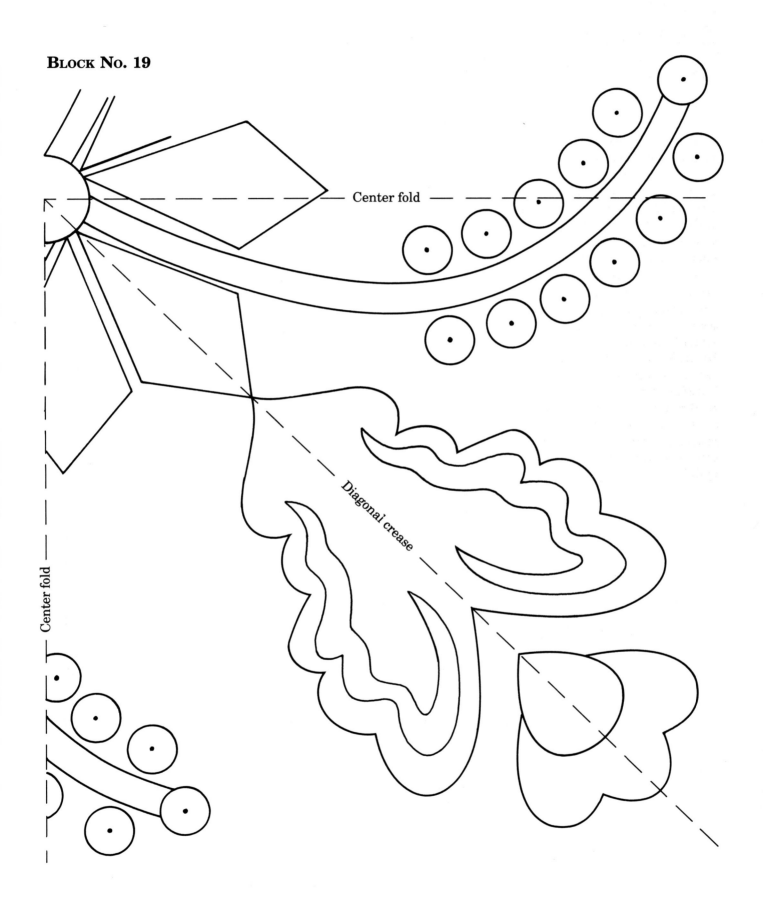

Center fold

Center fold

Diagonal crease

PINEAPPLE-POMEGRANATE

The Pineapple is an eighteenth- and nineteenth-century motif whose symbolism was conveyed with the same meaning in all design mediums. Whether carved onto a staircase or stitched into a quilt, it was clear to all that hospitality was being offered. This universal symbolism made the Pineapple a perfect choice for a front-bedroom, "best" appliqué quilt, and many were made for that purpose.

In quiltmaking, the Pineapple is depicted with two different basic arrangements: (1) a large, single fruit usually set diagonally on the block and (2) four mirror-image motifs that radiate from the center of the block toward each of the four outside corners. The large, single-fruit style is easily identified as a pineapple because it is detailed with pineapple features, such as a pieced sawtooth center that imitates the rough outside texture of the fruit and perhaps a large, spiny top section (see Sketches 1–7 on page 101).

When the "fruit" of the four-part Pineapple block was divided into slicelike sections, its name changed from "Pineapple" to "Pomegranate" (see Sketches 11–15). Traditionally, the name was further modified to "Love Apple" when one of the four fruits was separated and portrayed alone as a long-stemmed single motif (Sketch 16).

A full-size Pomegranate pattern is provided on pages 107–8, and an interesting 32" Pineapple pattern is given on pages 102–6.

PINEAPPLE, POMEGRANATE, AND LOVE APPLE SKETCHES

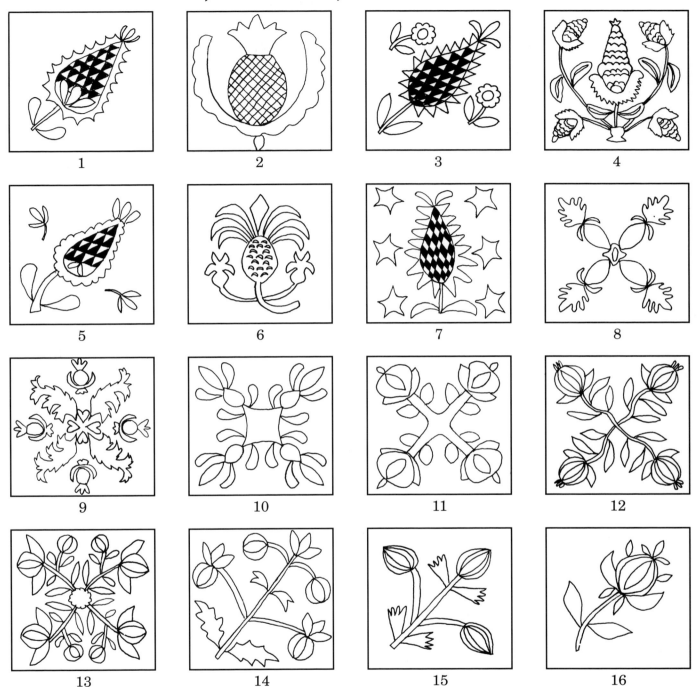

1. *Ruth E. Finley,* Old Patchwork Quilts and the Women Who Made Them, *Plate 80; 2. Marguerite Ickis,* The Standard Book of Quiltmaking and Collecting, *p. 82; 3. 1988 Quilt Engagement Calendar, Plate 53; 4. Robert Bishop,* New Discoveries in American Quilts, *p. 71; 5. Cyril I. Nelson and Carter Houck,* The Quilt Engagement Calendar Treasury, *p. 183; 6. Edwin Binney III and Gail Binney-Winslow,* Homage to Amanda: Two Hundred Years of American Quilts, *p. 47; 7. Quilt (Summer 1989), p. 29; 8. Sandi Fox,* Small Endearments, *p. 58; 9. Binney and Binney-Winslow,* Homage to Amanda, *p. 43; 10. MacDowell and Fitzgerald,* Michigan Quilts, *p. 29; 11. Marsha McCloskey,* Christmas Quilts, *p. 28; 12. Bettina Havig,* Missouri Heritage Quilts, *pp. 34–35; 13. Jeannette Lasansky,* In the Heart of Pennsylvania, *p. 37; 14. Carleton Safford and Robert Bishop,* America's Quilts and Coverlets, *p. 188; 15. Fox,* Small Endearments, *Plate 41; 16. Karoline Patterson Bresenhan and Nancy O'Bryant Puentes,* Lone Stars: A Legacy of Texas Quilts, 1836–1936, *pp. 32–33.*

BLOCK NO. 20
Pineapple/ Carnation Medallion

Finished Size: 32" x 32"

Of particular interest to me was the use of three design elements combined on five different nineteenth-century appliqué quilts and one quilted counterpane that I found while researching this book. These quilts were made in states covering a wide geographical area; however, several were made in Kentucky. The designs I found covered a sixty-year period. The three elements that all of these quilts have in common are: a carnation-type flower (sometimes called a "pink"), a Pineapple motif, and a Pomegranate or Love Apple motif. Two of the quilts are found on pages 25 and 130[29]. It is intriguing to me that these particular elements were combined in so many sepa-

(continued on page 103)

CONSTRUCTION

1. Cut paper for Master Pattern 32" square. The pattern sections given on pages 104–6 combine to make one-fourth of the full 32" design. Fold 32" paper pattern into fourths. Further divide the upper right quarter section of this paper into fourths by either folding or drawing with a pencil and ruler. The diagonal crease and center fold indication marks on the pattern sections indicate the center and sides of the upper right quarter section.

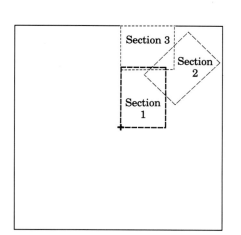

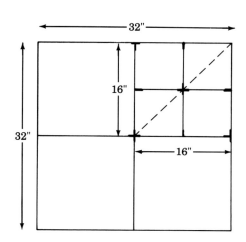

2. Trace Section 1 onto Master Pattern quarter section. (This makes one-fourth of large center flower, pineapple stem, and left carnation flower.) Next, trace Section 2. Trace the third pattern section onto upper left of quarter-section pattern (stem and simple flower). Fold the section just traced in half diagonally through the center (along pineapple stem and through pineapple). Trace mirror image of design elements just drawn (carnation and simple flower) onto opposite diagonal side to complete a quarter section of Master Pattern.

   Complete full Master Pattern by folding entire Master Pattern paper in half horizontally and tracing lower right section. Refold vertically and trace left side of block, completing the pattern.

3. Begin appliqué with large center rose. After appliqué of largest outside rose is complete, cut away the background fabric. (See instructions for Cutting Away Back of Appliqué on page 154.) After stitching each layer of the rose, cut away the previous layer where it is overlapped by appliqué just completed. This will reduce the bulk produced by several layers.

4. Appliqué double-leaf sections surrounding center rose. Before adding the third disjointed leaf to complete the triple leaf cluster, appliqué stem that is overlapped by leaf. Refer to Master Pattern before deciding which stem, either pineapple or double stems for carnations, to stitch.

5. Appliqué carnation flowers in the following order: (a) green flower base; (b) two center carnation petals; (c) next petals working away from center; and (d) lower carnation petals.

6. Appliqué Pineapple motif in the following order: (a) circle at base of stem; (b) scalloped sides of pineapple; (c) circles in center of pineapple; and (d) small leaf cluster at top of pineapple.

7. Appliqué outside vine before triple leaf sections and simple flowers that are arranged along vine.

(continued from page 102)

rate occasions. It may be that there is symbolism implied by using them together, but that significance is lost to us after so many years.

The following 32" pattern is a block that uses the Pineapple/Carnation motif. This motif can be used as a large central medallion, as seen on the sampler quilt on page 133, as a four-unit quilt, or by itself as a wall hanging. Annette Bracken stitched this pattern into a striking wall quilt, which can be seen on page 138.

BLOCK NO. 20
SECTION 1

Center fold

Diagonal crease

Center fold

**BLOCK NO. 20
SECTION 2**

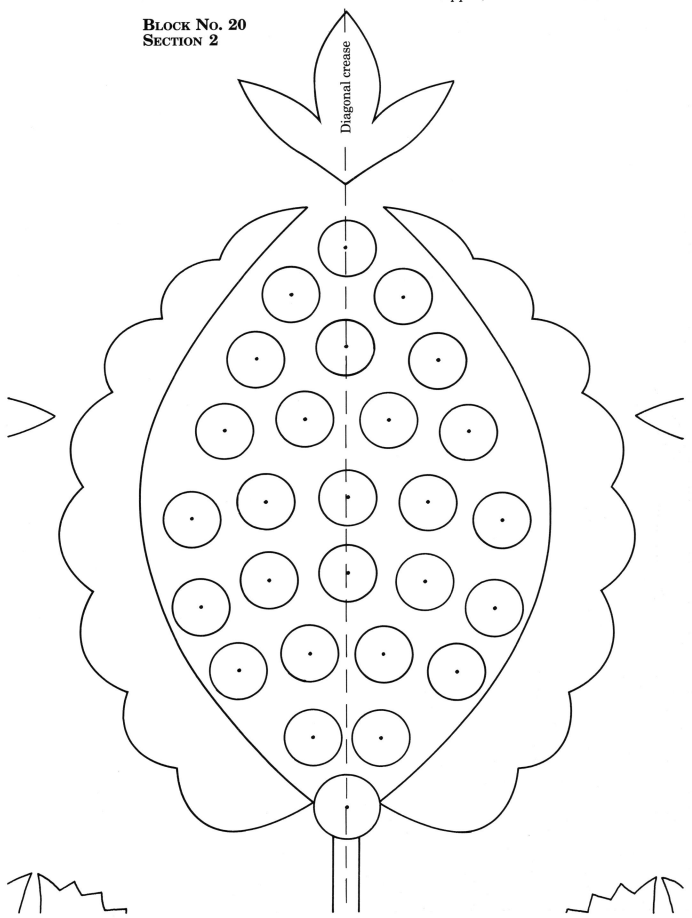

Diagonal crease

Center fold

BLOCK NO. 21
Pomegranate

Finished Size: 16" x 16"

This crossed branch–type design is similar to the four-section Pineapple format. The major difference in the two designs is that the body of the fruit in the Pomegranate pattern is appliquéd in "sliced" sections, while the pineapple fruit body is left whole.

As mentioned earlier, this pattern's name changes to "Love Apple" when one quarter section of the block is used as the entire block design. Should you want to adapt this pattern as a Love Apple design, enlarge or reduce the pattern section on page 108 to fit your chosen background fabric size, or use it in the size provided and cut your background fabric based on a 8" finished block size.

The full-size pattern given here is a fairly easy one to stitch and is a good beginner's block. The Pomegranate quilt on page 136 was Aileen Stannis's first appliqué quilt, and the finished result is beautiful.

CONSTRUCTION

1. Use the single pattern section on page 108 to make Master Pattern. First, trace the design onto the lower right section. Next, fold Master Pattern in half horizontally and trace upper right section. Refold vertically and trace left side of block, completing pattern.
2. Appliqué stems. Make bias that is ⅜" (finished width) x 22." (See Bias-Strip Construction method on page 155.) Cut bias in half and appliqué each of the two stems.
3. Appliqué pomegranate fruit in the following order: (a) green leaf base; (b) largest red fruit piece; (c) yellow center piece is placed as next layer so that it will be overlapped and raw edges completely concealed when outside petals are stitched); (d) two pink petals (appliqué over top of yellow center fabric); and (e) two-leaf detail at top of fruit.
4. Add leaves.

BLOCK NO. 21

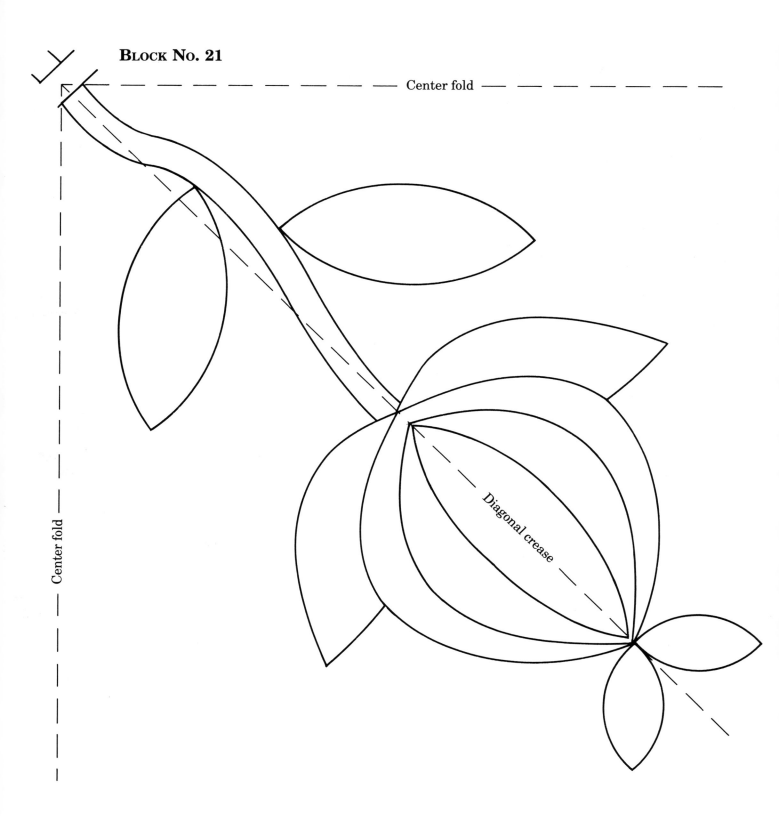

Center fold

Center fold

Diagonal crease

Oak Leaf

In general, appliqué designs that use a large amount of foliage seem masculine when compared to other floral appliqué topics. The sketches on page 110 and the pattern on page 111 seem to use foliage as the major design element, and they do have a masculine feel. In 1949, Marguerite Ickis confirmed the masculinity of this design type while discussing an Oak Leaf pattern in her book:

> A quilt of this pattern makes one of the best choices for use in a man's room; it has strength, dignity and simplicity in its flavor.[30]

The qualities of "strength, dignity and simplicity" make the Oak Leaf an appealing appliqué topic for any gender.

The ease with which the Oak Leaf can be stitched also makes it attractive. With its large pieces and lack of sharp points on the outside edges or between the "fingers" of the leaves, the Oak Leaf is easy even for a beginner.

Two unusual names assigned to the Oak Leaf design are "Hickory Leaf" and "Pumpkin Flower."

Oak Leaf and Foliage Sketches

1. 2. 3. 4.

5. 6. 7. 8.

9. 10. 11. 12.

13. 14. 15. 16.

1. Ruth E. Finley, Old Patchwork Quilts and the Women Who Made Them, *Plate 92; 2. Rita Barrow Barber,* Somewhere in Between Quilts and Quilters of Illinois, *p. 21; 3. Marguerite Ickis,* The Standard Book of Quiltmaking and Collecting, *p. 106; 4. Carrie A. Hall and Rose G. Kretsinger,* The Romance of the Patchwork Quilt in America, *p. 118; 5. Cyril I. Nelson and Carter Houck,* The Quilt Engagement Calendar Treasury, *p. 20; 6. Hall and Kretsinger,* The Romance of the Patchwork Quilt in America, *p. 108; 7. Carleton Safford and Robert Bishop,* America's Quilts and Coverlets, *p. 194; 8. Lady's Circle Patchwork Quilts* (Summer 1982), *p. 10; 9. Safford and Bishop,* America's Quilts and Coverlets, *p. 202; 10. Lady's Circle Patchwork Quilts* (Summer 1982), *p. 17; 11. Safford and Bishop,* America's Quilts and Coverlets, *p. 162; 12. Safford and Bishop,* America's Quilts and Coverlets, *p. 161; 13. Cincinnati Art Museum,* Quilts from Cincinnati Collections, *p. 34; 14. Sandi Fox,* Small Endearments, *p. 29; 15. Marsha MacDowell and Ruth D. Fitzgerald,* Michigan Quilts: 150 Years of a Textile Tradition, *p. 29; 16. Ickis,* The Standard Book of Quiltmaking and Collecting, *p. 55.*

BLOCK NO. 22
Oak Leaf and Acorn

Finished Size: 16" x 16"

This pattern combines three typical design elements of the Oak Leaf–type pattern: acorns, berries, and the large oak leaf. When Elna Johnson chose this pattern for her red-and-green appliqué quilt, she decided to substitute her favorite motif—the butterfly—for the berries. Her attractive quilt on page 138 features four different butterfly designs that she adapted to fit her appliqué block. Elna's one modification to this design gives the block a completely different look.

CONSTRUCTION

1. Use the single pattern section on page 112 to make Master Pattern. First, trace the design onto the lower right section. Next, fold Master Pattern in half horizontally and trace upper right section. Refold vertically and trace left side of block, completing pattern.
2. Stitch the small secondary stems first, followed by the large four-leaf oak piece. The reverse appliqué detail on the oak leaves is optional. (See Reverse Appliqué instructions on page 155–56).
3. Appliqué acorns. Appliqué the acorn body (yellow on color photo) before acorn cap (red).
4. Add the leaves and berries.

BLOCK NO. 22

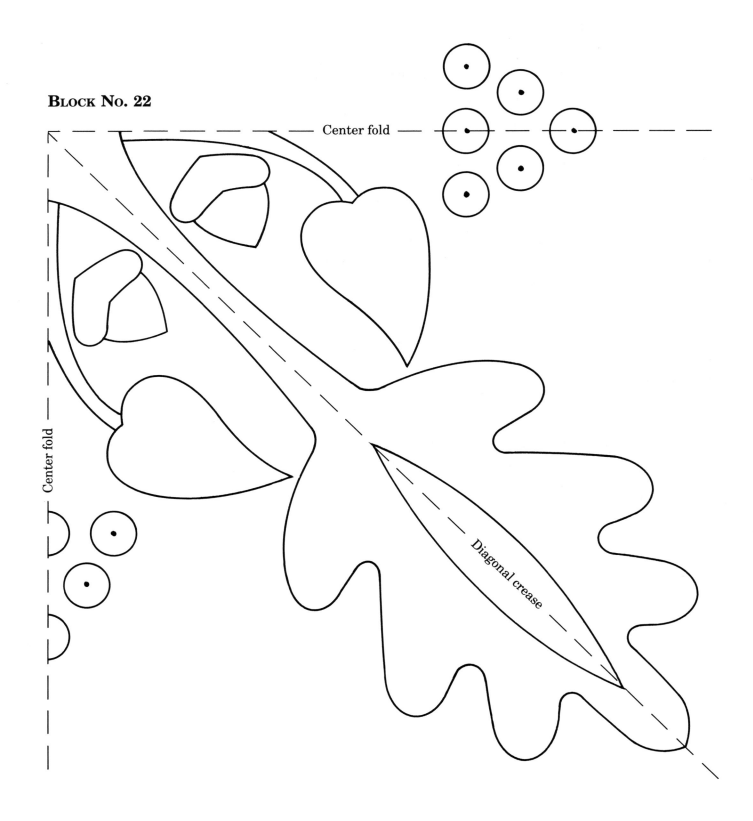

Center fold

Center fold

Diagonal crease

Original Designs

The majority of the quilts in this category feature baskets or pots of flowers arranged by the quilts' makers in individualized designs. No two of them are alike; some are symmetrical and perfectly balanced, while others contain flowers that seem to have been randomly placed. Since each quilt is unique to its maker, each makes a personal statement about the person who made it. It is interesting to study a quilt and speculate about the woman who designed and stitched each piece. The sketches on page 114 show sixteen original designs.

Included in this category are triple flower designs. These blocks are typically set "on point," with three large flowers balancing three of the corners and their stems "growing" from the fourth corner. Each of the triple flower quilts I found used different flower motifs. Sketches 12–14 are original versions of the familiar Tree of Life theme.

The last two sketches are original renderings of giant strawberries. The full-size quilt containing the block shown in Sketch 16 had only five blocks and no borders. Sketch 15 shows the block repeated only nine times to make up a 92" x 90" quilt with a small, plain outside border.

The two full-size patterns given in this section are reproductions of one-of-a-kind quilts, which I was able to study closely in person. The original quilts that these blocks came from were so expertly executed that I felt compelled to try just one block to share the perfection evidenced in these two quiltmakers' work. Perhaps you will want to do the same or reproduce an entire quilt.

ORIGINAL DESIGN SKETCHES

1. *Carrie A. Hall and Rose G. Kretsinger,* The Romance of the Patchwork Quilt in America, *p. 186; 2. Hall and Kretsinger,* The Romance of the Patchwork Quilt in America, *p. 198; 3.* Quilt Digest 3 (1985), *p. 49; 4. Sandi Fox,* Small Endearments, *Plate 42; 5.* 1985 Quilt Engagement Calendar, *Plate 39. 6. Carleton Safford and Robert Bishop,* America's Quilts and Coverlets, *p.190; 7. Jeannette Lasansky,* In the Heart of Pennsylvania, *p. 38; 8. Safford and Bishop,* America's Quilts and Coverlets, *p. 164; 9. Bets Ramsey and Merikay Waldvogel,* The Quilts of Tennessee, *p. 42; 10. Karoline Patterson Bresenhan and Nancy O'Bryant Puentes,* Lone Stars: A Legacy of Texas Quilts, 1836–1936, *p. 75; 11.* 1986 Quilt Engagement Calendar, *Plate 27; 12. Bresenhan and Puentes,* Lone Stars, *pp. 36–37; 13. Ramsey and Waldvogel,* The Quilts of Tennessee, *pp. 50–51; 14.* 1988 Quilt Engagement Calendar, *Plate 46; 15. Phyllis Haders,* The Warner Collector's Guide to American Quilts, *p. 220; 16. Hall and Kretsinger,* The Romance of the Patchwork Quilt in America, *p. 167.*

CONSTRUCTION

1. There are three pattern sections used in this block on pages 116–18. Beginning with Section No. 3 on page 118, trace the base of the main stem and the lower branches along it. Using diagonal crease and center fold indication marks as guides, position and trace the other two pattern sections. Fold Master Pattern diagonally along center vine and trace the mirror image onto left side, completing pattern.
2. Appliqué stems first. Begin with the smallest berry and leaf stems, then add the side stems and the main center stem. If desired, the smallest stems and the side stems can be cut out and appliquéd as one piece instead of several separate pieces.
3. Appliqué the three roses in layers, beginning with the largest layer and continuing to flower center. After each layer is appliquéd, cut away the previous layer where it is overlapped by layer just sewn. This will reduce bulk produced by several layers.
4. Add berries. Begin stitching each group of berries with the berry that covers stem end and work back along sides of stem toward main branch.
5. Stitch leaves. Slight adjustments may be necessary to ensure that they do not overlap onto any of the berries or flowers.

BLOCK NO. 23
Mary L. Coray Floral with Berries

Finished Size: 16" x 16"

A full view of this exceptional quilt is seen on page 143. There are 110 perfectly stuffed berries on each of the original quilt's blocks, totaling more than one thousand berries on the entire quilt. The berries on this version of the quilt block have not been stuffed. This quiltmaker must have felt that her quilt's best feature was the quilting. A record came with the quilt as follows: "Seventeen hundred yards of thread were used in quilting the peony design and 1,000 in the grape design." This information was carefully relayed with the quilt when it was donated to the L.D.S. Church Museum of History and Art.

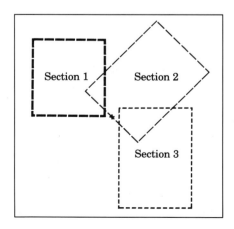

BLOCK NO. 23
SECTION 1

Diagonal crease

Center fold

BLOCK No. 23
SECTION 2

Diagonal crease

Center fold

Center fold

BLOCK NO. 23
SECTION 3

Center fold

Diagonal crease

BLOCK NO. 24
L. R. H. Rose Vase

Finished Size: 16" x 16"

A full-color photo as well as close-ups of this original quilt are shown on pages 29 and 31. The story of this quilt's discovery and a detailed description of its features are also given on pages 28–31. After having appliquéd the serrated-edged leaves on this block, I have renewed respect for its maker. This block is difficult and not recommended as a first appliqué effort.

CONSTRUCTION

1. There are three pattern sections used in this block on pages 121–23. Beginning with Section No. 3 on page 123, trace the vase, main stem, and lower branches along it. Using diagonal crease and center fold indication marks as guides, position and trace the other two pattern sections. Fold Master Pattern diagonally along center vine and trace the mirror image onto left side, completing pattern.

2. Appliqué stems. Begin with the smallest berry and leaf stems, then add the side stems and the main center stem. If desired, the smallest stems and the side stems can be cut out and appliquéd as one piece instead of several separate pieces.

3. Begin center rose appliqué with green flower base, then add the center rose upon base in layers. After each rose layer is appliquéd, cut away the previous layer where it is overlapped by layer just sewn. This will reduce bulk produced by several layers.

4. Appliqué the following motifs in order listed: (a) top bud; (b) outside simple flowers; and (c) vase.

5. Appliqué the leaves and berries. Slight adjustments may be required to make them fit into the design without overlapping onto any of the other motifs. Begin appliqué of berries with the ones that cover stem ends. Layer remaining berries in rows to create organized berry clusters. To accurately reproduce

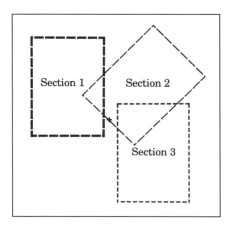

L. R. H.'s quilt, attach the leaves with buttonhole stitches placed solidly around the outside edge of each leaf; or appliqué with the needle-turn method as shown here. (See the closeup photo of L. R. H.'s buttonhole stitching on page 29 for example of how closely buttonhole embroidery stitches should be placed.) Instructions for buttonhole embroidery stitches are on page 36.

BLOCK NO. 24
SECTION 1

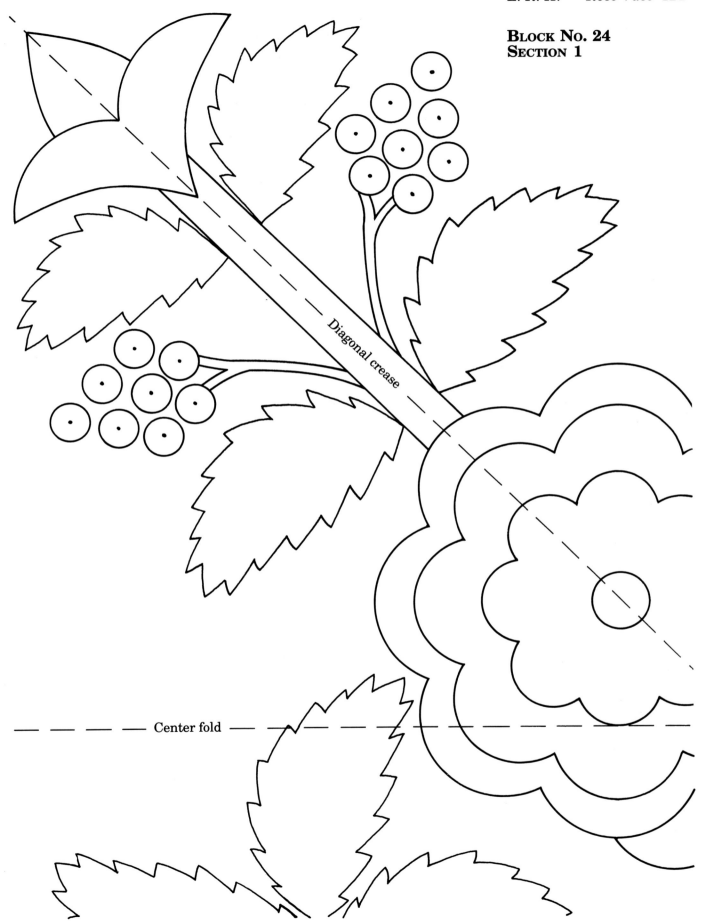

Diagonal crease

Center fold

BLOCK NO. 24
SECTION 2

Diagonal crease

Center fold

Center fold

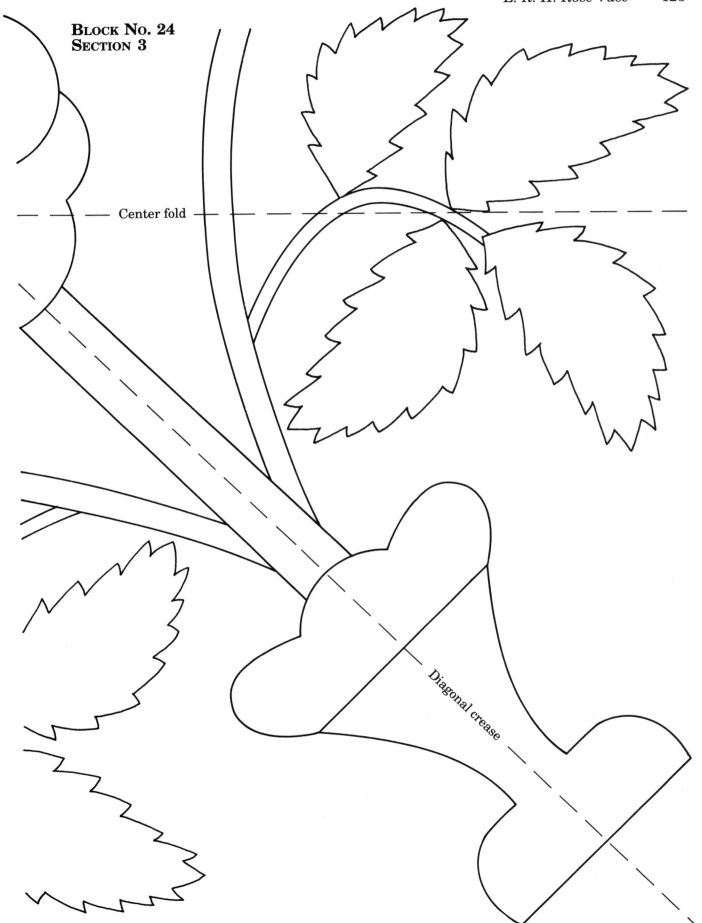

**BLOCK NO. 24
SECTION 3**

Center fold

Diagonal crease

Borders

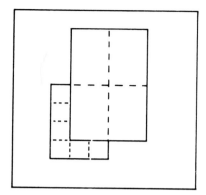

Step 1

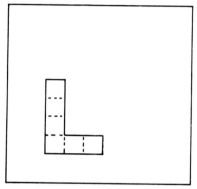

Step 2

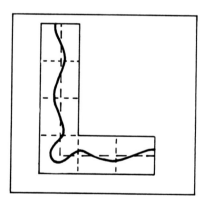

Step 3

The outside border of appliqué quilts serves two purposes: to contain the design developed with center blocks and to echo and/or complement motifs used in the center of the quilt, giving the whole quilt a feeling of continuity and balance.

The best way to add a border to a quilt is to customize it to fit the quilt top, since rarely do two quilt tops using the same blocks turn out the same size or have the same feel. Also, each quilt-maker will feel differently about what is most appropriate for her quilt.

There is one full-size border pattern given here, as well as many appliquéd versions shown in the Gallery on pages 129–47. These can be drawn to the size needed to fit your finished piece. The directions given below explain how to plan and divide the border into manageable proportions for designing or reproducing the border for your quilt.

Enlarging Borders

The appliqué borders pictured in this book can be drawn to fit your quilt by following these simple steps:

1. Make a paper pattern that equals one quarter section of the finished border of your quilt.
2. Fold the pattern paper into equal sections.
3. For a vine with flowers arranged along it, draw a vine that flows evenly through the divided sections.
4. Arrange the flowers and leaves along the vine, using a consistent amount of flowers and leaves in each section.
5. For a swag border, draw a swag that will fit between fold lines to fill each "section." Modify the swag piece to make it turn the corner in the corner sections.

See pages 149–51 for directions on drawing appliqué motifs to full size for your border.

I designed this 51" x 51" wall quilt in February 1987. Valentine's Day and hope for an early spring inspired its heart and tulip theme. Perhaps you can ward off the gloom of next winter by stitching one for yourself. The three 12" blocks used in this design are found on pages 71–76. The border pattern for "Bride of Tulip Valley" is found on pages 127–28. This quilt is an easy appliqué to stitch and would be just right for a beginner.

The three blocks used in "Bride of Tulip Valley" are 12" square. These three patterns are the only ones in the book based on a 12" block. Make Master Patterns for each block as described in the Construction section for these blocks.

Bride of Tulip Valley Quilt

CONSTRUCTION

1. Cut nine blocks that are 14" square (they are cut down to 12½" after appliqué is complete) from background fabric.
2. Make four Hearts and Tulips blocks (page 71), four Crossed Branches blocks (page 73), and one Heart Wreath block (page 75), as described in Construction section of each block.
3. After all blocks are appliquéd, cut background fabric down to 12½" square. Arrange and join blocks together as shown in color photo.
4. Cut four border strips that are 57" long and 9" wide.
5. Attach border strips; miter corners.
6. Patterns for appliqué swag border are on pages 127–28.
7. Mark for placement of border swags as follows: Begin at inside corner of border. Measure toward outside raw edges of quilt 2⅞" and mark with a dot. Measure 9" along seam that joins block to border, then measure down 2⅞" as before and mark dot (see illustration on page 127). Repeat the marking process around quilt border, beginning and ending at corner on each side where corner swag piece meets border swag piece. Depending on the accuracy of your quilt top construction, you may need to make slight adjustments in placement of swags, but the shape of the swag makes it easy to adjust the size as needed.
8. Appliqué swags, hearts, and leaves to background fabric, making points of swags meet at dots.

Border (detail) of Bride of Tulip Valley quilt

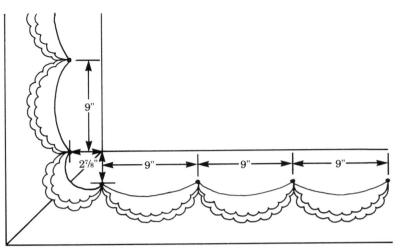

Mark for border swags

BRIDE OF TULIP VALLEY BORDER
SECTION 1

– – – – – – Dotted line indicates quilting

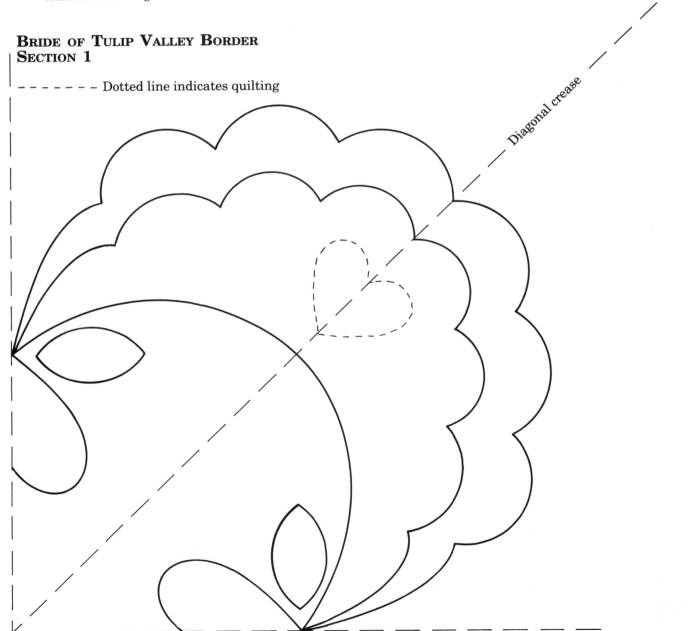

BRIDE OF TULIP VALLEY BORDER
SECTION 2

– – – – – – – Dotted line indicates quilting

Gallery

Red and Green Garden, Eleanor Tracy, 1990, West Valley, Utah, 106" x 90". Eleanor stitched all twenty of the 16" blocks from this book to make a magnificent full-size quilt. The simple swag border effectively frames and finishes the block collection. (Collection of Eleanor Tracy)

Pineapple Appliqué, Lucy Kemper West, c. 1860, Garrard County, Kentucky, 77¹/₄" x 74¹/₄". The pineapple, carnation, and pomegranate are combined in another unique arrangement. Design possibilities are limitless even when using the same subjects, as can be seen by the two other quilts (pages 25 and 138) with the same combination of elements. (Photo courtesy of DAR Museum, Washington, D.C., Acc. no. 85.6)

Stylized Tulip, Margaret Jane McMath, c. 1850, Rockbridge County, Virginia, 94¹/₂" x 87¹/₂". The tulip was a favorite appliqué topic of many nineteenth- and early twentieth-century quiltmakers. This version is especially charming, with its unusual wide sashing between the blocks showcasing each block. A hand print, which may have been traced from the quiltmaker's own hand, is quilted in each corner. (Photo courtesy of DAR Museum, Washington, D.C., Acc. no. 78.29)

Harrison Rose Urn, Susan Noakes McCord, c. 1860, McCordsville, Indiana, 81" x 76¹/₂". The large flower in the center of the urn was identified as the "Harrison Rose." The Harrison Rose was named for Indiana territory's first governor and ninth U.S. president, William Henry Harrison. Notice how Susan cleverly avoided turning any corners with her outside vine border by changing the major flower motifs on each side. (From the collections of Henry Ford Museum & Greenfield Village, Dearborn, Michigan, Neg. no. 24-A-3)

Red and Green Sampler, Jeana Kimball, 1990, Salt Lake City, Utah, 76" x 76". Thirteen blocks from this book are combined to make a lovely sampler quilt. The blocks are set together with a narrow red border that carries the color scheme to the outside edges of the quilt. (Collection of the author)

*Hexagon Rose Wreath,
Jeana Kimball, 1990, Salt
Lake City, Utah, 79" x 79".
The rose used in an 1842
red-and-green appliqué
quilt inspired this four-
block quilt. What began as
an attraction to one ap-
pliqué flower blossomed into an
entire book. (Quilted by Loraine H.
Jones; collection of the author)*

Asymmetrical Rose with Swag Border (above, left), Beth Crawford, 1990, Salt Lake City, Utah, 53" x 53". The pleasing circular arrangement of the four blocks is one of many possibilities for the layout of this quilt. The scalloped swag adds just the right touch to frame and set off this quilt. (Collection of Beth Crawford)

Whig Rose (above, right), Maureen Blosch, 1989, West Valley City, Utah, 30^1/$_2$" x 30^1/$_2$". One Whig Rose block has been set off beautifully with Maureen's unusual border treatment. (Collection of Maureen Blosch)

Bind It Again, Sam (left), Kristine Haas, 1990, Orem, Utah, 42" x 42". The Tulip Basket block is bordered with a chain of pieced Tiny Basket blocks and then beautifully quilted with tulips, feathers, and cross-hatching. This quilt earned its name after the binding was reapplied for the third time. (Collection of Kristine Haas)

Oak Leaf and Reel, made by friends of Benjamin B. and Martha Allice Clark Pierce, c. 1860–1861, New Jersey, 86" x 84". The blocks of this friendship and memory quilt were stitched by friends of the young couple when they became engaged to be married. The young men bought the fabrics needed for the blocks, and the ladies stitched them together. Before the quilt was finished, the Civil War was declared. Benjamin returned from the war and they were married, but many of their friends were not so lucky. Most Oak Leaf and Reel quilts combine the two elements into one block, but this quilt uses the design elements as two separate blocks. (Private collection, Boise, Idaho)

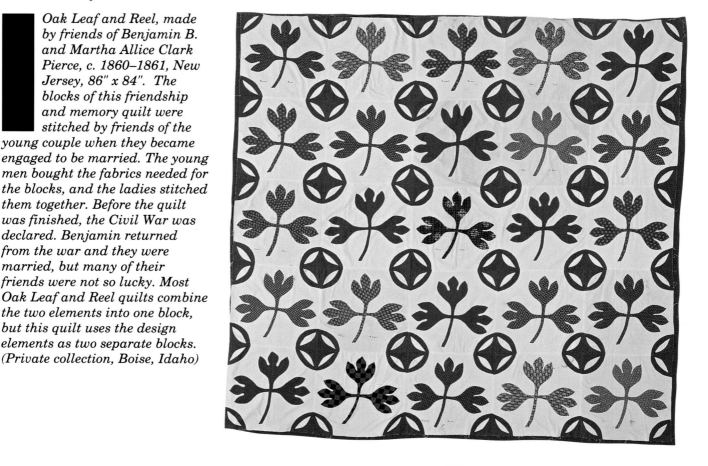

Pomegranate, Aileen Stannis, 1988, Berkley, Michigan, 108" x 90". This gorgeous quilt was Aileen's first appliqué quilt. "Best of Show" at the Great Lakes Biennial Quilt Show in 1988 is just one of the honors it has received.

Tulips, maker unknown, 1840–1850, Hagerstown, Maryland, 90" x 88". The center circle vine and curved stems give this vibrant quilt a feel of organized motion. The appliquéd feathered vine border was a perfect choice to complement the bold arrangement. Notice how the feathered border keeps the quilt from becoming "dizzy" by reversing the direction of the circling tulips. (Photo courtesy of America Hurrah Antiques, New York City)

Appliqué Cradle quilt, Mrs. L. A. Seaton, c. 1860, Troy, Missouri, 37" x 37". This original-design appliqué baby quilt was used by several generations of babies in Mrs. Seaton's family. Also handed down with the quilt was information that the fabric used to make this quilt was purchased for $1.00 per yard. (Collection of Daughters of Utah Pioneers Museum, Salt Lake City, Utah; photo by Borge Andersen)

Pineapple for Elise (above, left), Annette Bracken, 1990, West Jordan, Utah, 56" x 53^1/$_2$". The unusual yellow gold–and red color scheme are very effective for this subject matter. Note how the Pineapple motif was modified to a smaller size for the border. (Collection of Annette Bracken)

Victorian Rose (above, right), Minerva Colemere, 1990, Salt Lake City, Utah, 54" x 54". The soft colors and gentle curves make this a wonderfully feminine quilt. The vine border expands to fill in the half- and quarter-blocks used to square off the on-point setting of these blocks. (Collection of Minerva Colemere)

Gifts from Nature (right), Elna Johnson, 1990, Salt Lake City, Utah, 54" x 54". The four Oak Leaf blocks are traced with a vine that forms four secondary leaf shapes. Elna's addition of four Butterfly motifs gives the Oak Leaf block an added dimension. (Collection of Elna Johnson)

Grace's Quail, Kristine Haas, 1990, Orem, Utah, 65" x 65". The cockscomb flower is accented with happy little birds and plump berries. The pieced flying geese on the inside border enhance the flowers and birds and give the quilt a bold feel. (Collection of Kristine Haas)

Rose with Vine Border, Connie Sheffield, 1984, Salt Lake City, Utah, 58" x 58". A combination of pieced and appliqué borders sets off the lovely appliqué block in the center. (Collection of Connie Sheffield)

Thistle, Jane Grady Duncan, c. 1850, Springfield, Illinois, 94" x 89". This quilt was cleverly constructed in two parts to ensure that none of the appliqué design would be lost by being tucked under pillows. Quilted in the 1920s or 1930s by Ann Black Mellinger. (Photo courtesy of L.D.S. Church Museum of History and Art, Salt Lake City, Utah)

Floral Urn, Susan Noakes McCord, c. 1860, McCordsville, Indiana, 85¹/₂" x 80". The urn contains a whimsical collection of tulip-type motifs. Many of the leaves are strip pieced, a typical feature on several of Susan McCord's quilts. Notice how the four borders have the same "skeleton" but different flower motifs, with buds or berries arranged along them. (From the collections of Henry Ford Museum & Greenfield Village, Dearborn, Michigan, Neg. no. 24-A-11)

Asymmetrical Rose,
Elizabeth Shank, 1842,
Rogerville, Ohio, 81" x 79".
The Rose motif used on
this quilt is unusual
because it is based on a
hexagon for the flower
center. The border repeats
a smaller version of the hexagon
center rose. See page 135 for a
quilt that was inspired by this
unusual flower. (Collection of the
Daughters of Utah Pioneers
Museum, Salt Lake City, Utah;
photo by Borge Andersen)

Cockscomb, origin unknown, c. 1850, 86" x 86". This four-block quilt is especially appealing with its vibrant colors and bold design. The border echoes the Cockscomb motif on a smaller scale. (Photo courtesy of Thomas K. Woodard: American Antiques & Quilts)

Triple Flowers Set On Point, Mary E. Lusk Coray, c. 1855–1860, Missouri, 82" x 73". A masterpiece quilt that boasts 2,700 yards of thread in its quilting. Note the center block where the colors in the main flowers were changed. (Photo courtesy of L.D.S. Church Museum of History and Art, Salt Lake City, Utah)

Oak Leaves with Cherries, origin unknown, c. 1865, 80" x 76". This joyful quilt looks as if it were designed for a wall instead of a bed, an idea that would have been highly unusual for the nineteenth century. It was skillfully planned in both color and design, giving it perfect balance. (Photo courtesy of Thomas K. Woodard: American Antiques & Quilts)

Ruched Rose Wreath, made by the female members of the Sheetz Family, 1860, Cooksville, Howard County, Maryland, 96" x 96". All of the Rose motifs are stitched in the ruching techniques. It is believed that this quilt was made for seven-year-old Winfield Augustus Sheetz by his mother and her sisters. (Photo courtesy of DAR Museum, Washington, D.C., Acc. no. 89.13)

Single Stem Rose, made by the mother and sisters of Mary Ann Poindexter Staples, 1852, Missouri, 104" x 83³/₈". Made as a wedding quilt, this beautifully designed quilt is also expertly quilted, including stuffed doves between all of the Rose blocks. (Photo courtesy of DAR Museum, Washington D.C., Acc. no. 88.61)

Single Stem Rose variation, maker unknown, c. 1850, southern states, 83" x 83". What appears to be a four-block quilt is actually four smaller blocks combined to make each quarter section. The border is cleverly designed and expertly executed. This quiltmaker successfully introduced several new elements in her border by repeating the same fabrics and including a smaller scale, eight-petal rose with bud from the center design. (Collection of Jean C. Christensen, Salt Lake City, Utah; photo by Borge Andersen)

Rose of Sharon, maker unknown, c. 1850–1860, southern states, 82" x 77". The sixteen blocks are cleverly set together with a single rose. That same rose appears again in the border on a vine. Each basket holds a single daisy and two iris-like flowers. (Collection of Jean C. Christensen, Salt Lake City, Utah; photo by Borg Andersen)

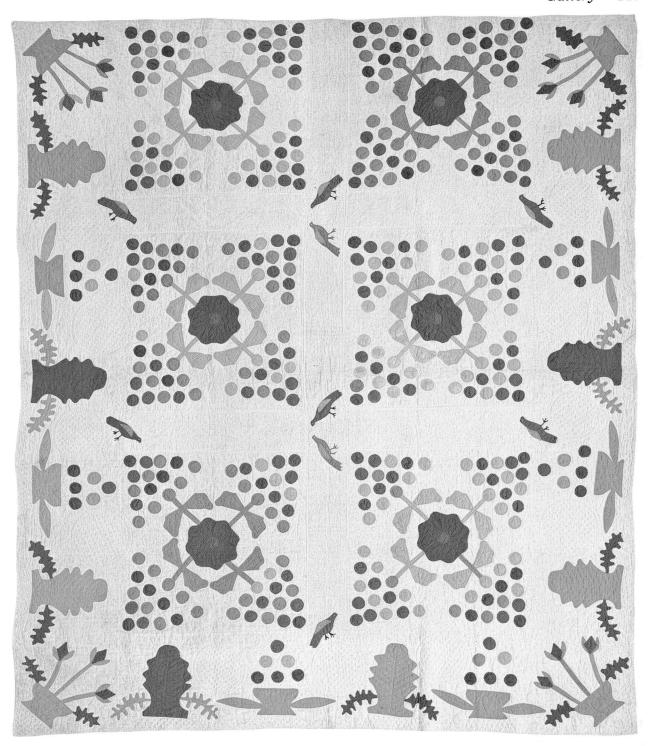

Cherry, origin unknown, c. 1850. All of the pink fabric on this quilt was a replacement of the previous color (probably red). While applying the new pink fabric, the seamstress altered the original design by placing the center flower over each set of crossed stems. The quilt owner must have truly loved this quilt to have spent so much time in updating it to her taste. (Collection of Judy Roche, Solebury, Pennsylvania)

Glossary of Techniques

Design Ideas

The designs you select to stitch in your quilts should be chosen the same way you choose other things for yourself, such as clothes and jewelry. You are influenced by what you already are, what you would like to be, and what you are becoming. Let those same factors influence you in the design of your appliqué quilt.

Choose design types that reflect your personality. Are you a detail person? If so, designs that are complex and intricate may be your choice. Do you like to make a bold statement with your clothes? Choosing a simple graphic design may be for you. Are you a gentle, soft-spoken person? The quiet curves of a Prairie Flower block may suit your taste. Or maybe you have a Jekyll-and-Hyde personality; if so, let your quilt reflect your hidden self.

Choose colors that reflect your mood. One of my students began quilting while suffering from depression. Her fabric choices always included black. While being treated for and overcoming that depression, her quilt was her contact with reality and helped her work through a most difficult time in her life. Even though she has recovered, she continues to use small amounts of black in her quilts because black now represents her triumphant recovery, and she likes the drama it adds to her work.

The main thing to remember is to make the choices for yourself, not to please anyone else. You may want input from others, but remember the final decision is yours.

BASIC ARRANGEMENTS

Appliqué designs are categorized into six basic arrangements:

1. Circular or wreath (see page 38 for sketches of this design type).
2. Foundation flower with radiating secondary parts (see pages 45 and 51).
3. Crossed branches (see pages 67 and 78).
4. Triple branch growing from a corner and usually set "on point" (see pages 101 and 114).
5. Arrangements of various flowers in a container (see pages 78 and 114).
6. Asymmetrical arrangement (see page 57).

SELECTING DESIGN COMPONENTS

Select one of the above basic arrangements and then decide what design elements you will use to dress and fill your skeleton arrangement. To choose the flowers and leaves for your quilt, take some time and study closely all of the sketches and patterns given here for shapes that appeal to you. Also, look through your own library for other appliqué elements to aid in your research. While looking at each quilt or block that you like, ask yourself these questions:

1. What is my favorite part of this design?
2. Would it work as the main flower, or is it more appropriate for a secondary role, such as a smaller flower or bud?
3. What other motifs could I use with this quilt that would complement and set it off in a way that pleases me?

Chances are you will end up with more good candidates or ideas than you can possibly use on one quilt, which is all the better because your next quilt will already be started.

When planning the setting for your blocks and the border for your quilt, go through the same exercise, looking for quilt layouts and borders you like. The setting and border do not need to be completely planned ahead. Complete each phase and then study what you have done to decide what block setting or border arrangement will best enhance your quilt.

BACKGROUND SIZE

Now you are ready to start the construction of your Master Pattern.

Choose the size of your background. For a multiblock appliqué quilt I prefer a 16"-square block size. This size allows for a lot of detail that can be drawn to a manageable size for appliqué.

Simple designs are more appealing on a smaller background. "Bride of Tulip Valley" (page 125) has simple shapes with less detail and is more appropriate for a smaller background. A 12" size worked well for the blocks in that quilt. Also, a single-stem design, such as a single Tulip or Love Apple, would be more effective on a small, rather than a large, background fabric.

An ambitious design, such as the Pineapple/Carnation block (page 102), is much easier drawn and stitched on a large (32" square) background. Multiple major design elements combined on one block are best managed on a large background.

Once the background size has been chosen, cut a paper pattern the finished size of your block. Fold this paper pattern into fourths. Unfold it and fold again diagonally (from corner to corner across the middle) in both directions.

Using a pencil, ruler, compass, or folds of your paper pattern as measuring devices, sketch in the skeleton of your design.

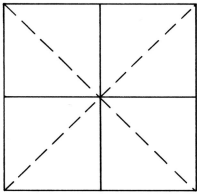

Fold paper pattern as shown

MAKING PATTERN PIECES

You are now ready to start adding design components to fill out your block. The best way to proceed is with scratch paper and scissors. You will find that you can cut much smoother lines and curves with scissors than you can draw with a pencil. Use a small pair of scissors that fits comfortably in your hand, such as 5" craft scissors. Large 8" scissors are bulky and more difficult to work with than a smaller pair.

Below are instructions for cutting out three basic "rose" motifs, which are the foundation for the majority of flowers on red-and-green quilts.

Begin by cutting out several 3" paper circles. Set your compass at 1½" and draw several circles; cut them out. Since your rose may need to be larger or smaller than 3" across, adjust the size of your circle to the size of your finished rose. Make circle ¼" to ½" larger than desired finished size to allow for trimming and shaping of petals. Using the circles you have just prepared, fold and cut as illustrated below to make the desired number of scalloped petals on your foundation flower.

EIGHT-PETAL FLOWER

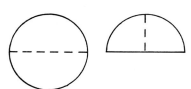

Measure and mark equal distance on each side

Cut rounded shape

Refold and recut as necessary to make petal definition suitable

SIX-PETAL FLOWER

Divide and fold into three equal sections

Measure and mark equal distance on each side

Cut rounded shape

Refold and recut as necessary to make petal definition suitable

FIVE- OR TEN-PETAL FLOWER

Fold in three divisions as shown

For ten-petal flower, fold one more time through center

Measure and mark equal distance on each side

Cut rounded shape

Refold and cut as necessary to make petal definition suitable

If you want your flowers to have pointed petals instead of rounded ones, cut straight lines in the place of rounded ones.

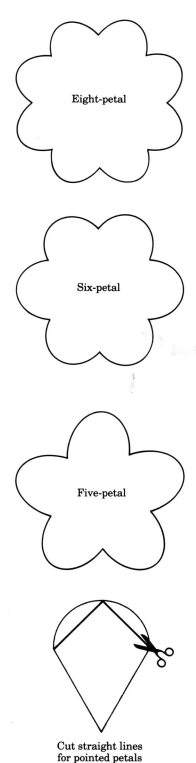

Eight-petal

Six-petal

Five-petal

Cut straight lines for pointed petals

Leaves and buds are easily shaped by cutting a mirror image with just one paper fold. Sketch the basic shape the motif should be and then cut out, smoothing and reshaping with the scissors as needed.

If the cutout design is not quite right, (1) fold another piece of scrap paper; (2) trace half of the previous design onto it; (3) sketch with a pencil an improved design; and (4) cut again along the new pencil line. Trace and recut as many times as necessary to get the correct shape and size for your design.

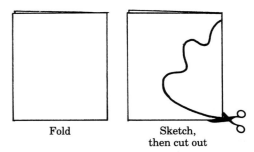

Fold   Sketch,
then cut out

Should your cutout motif be the exact shape you need, but you are unable to get the size right, enlarge or reduce your motif several times wih a photocopy machine. Leave the photocopy machine cover open so that the shapes are well defined against a black background. Adjust the reduction or enlargement from 5% to 10% increments each time you reduce or enlarge. One of the several sizes you try should fit your needs perfectly.

Pattern Layout

Experiment with the placement and arrangement of the cutout motifs you have just created. Move them around, trying the placement several ways before making a final decision on where they fit. You will know when it is right, because it will look right to you. If you struggle for some time without a solution, leave your work and return later. It is like working on a jigsaw puzzle. When you return, the perfect arrangement may be right there; you just did not see it before. Pencil in the block design and leave it overnight. If you are still pleased the next day, trace your design with a black marking pen and start your color and fabric selection. The more design work you do, the easier it becomes.

One final hint for the timid: Start small. Make small revisions to a full-size design, such as adding an extra layer to a flower, or adding or subtracting a leaf or bud. Each time you make a revision that is successful, you will be encouraged to continue with larger modifications. Before you know it, you will be designing your own one-of-a-kind appliqué quilts.

Needle-Turn Appliqué

The needle-turn method of appliqué is one in which the needle is used as a tool to turn under the raw edge of fabric as you stitch. This method provides a smooth, clean edge and, with a little practice, becomes quick and easy to use. The need for time-consuming basting is completely eliminated, but a little extra care is needed to make sure the appliqué pieces are positioned correctly before beginning to stitch.

Since the needle is such an important part of this method, a long, fine needle is highly recommended: size 11, Sharp.

1. Using thread color that matches appliqué piece, cut an 18" length to work with. If the thread is too long, it tends to knot

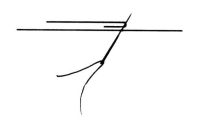

and tangle. Cut thread on an angle to assist in threading into the small eye of the size 11 Sharp needle.

2. Tie a knot in the end of the thread. To make a small, firm knot that will not come loose, use the following procedure:

   Holding the threaded needle in your right hand, between thumb and forefinger, and the tail of the thread in your left hand, point them toward each other. Grasp end of thread in fingers holding needle, then use left hand to wrap thread around needle four or five times. Hold the wraps with right thumb and forefinger and pull the needle through the wraps with left hand. Hold the wraps tightly until thread is pulled all the way through. You will have a small, firm knot, similar to a French knot. Don't be concerned if there is a bit of a tail; just cut it off.

3. Position the appliqué piece to the spot it is to be applied by putting a pin through the pencil-marked point where it should touch an adjoining piece. For example, it is best to first pin a leaf through the point where it will touch the stem. This is important, since the raw edges have not yet been turned under, and it is difficult to determine the exact placement. Pin in place with an adequate number of pins, but don't pin too heavily as the pins will get in the way and catch the thread during stitching. Example: a simple, small leaf requires two pins.

4. It is important to begin stitching on the straightest edge possible and as close to the point where the piece being appliquéd touches an adjoining piece. If you are right-handed, stitch counterclockwise; if you are left-handed, stitch clockwise.

   Begin by using the threaded needle to catch and turn under the seam allowance that has been marked on the right side of fabric. Once seam allowance is turned under, use left thumbnail (or tip of thumb) on the top and second finger of left hand underneath fabric as a clamp to hold turned-under seam allowance in place as you stitch; this helps ensure a smooth edge.

   Take first stitch by bringing needle up through the background fabric, through the seam allowance that has been turned under, and out through the fold of the piece being appliquéd. Pull needle up and through so that you are now working on the top of the fabric only, and the knot is left underneath, on the wrong side of background fabric.

   Make next stitch by inserting needle into background fabric only, immediately next to first stitch. (The tip of the needle is now touching your fingers underneath the piece.) Turn the needle horizontally, travel along approximately $1/16$" on the wrong side of the background fabric, and then bring needle straight up (through the background fabric and through the fold) as before. Do not slant needle when going in or out of the fabric; appliquéd edge will not lie flat and stitches may show on top. Stitches should be invisible on top; only slight indentations, where stitches have been taken, should be visible. Give thread a little tug every three or four stitches to further anchor stitches.

Continue stitching this way, spacing the stitches approximately ¹⁄₁₆" apart. The wrong side of background fabric should show even spans of thread, with only a tiny gap where the thread has gone through to the top to take a "bite" out of the fold.

Two problem spots that are encountered in appliqué are making sharp points and keeping inverted points from fraying. The following are techniques to solve these problems.

Making Points Sharp. Stitch in the method described earlier, along the edge of the piece and right up to the point of the piece, taking last stitch in pencil-marked point. Turn entire block so appliqué will progress in the proper direction (counterclockwise if you are right-handed, clockwise if you are left-handed). Using fine, sharp scissors, trim excess seam allowance; then using the needle as a tool, turn and tuck under seam allowance. If the point of the piece gets pushed under in the process of turning seam allowance, give a little tug to the thread and the point will pop back out into place. After seam allowance has been turned satisfactorily, take next stitch going away from point and proceed as normal.

The secret of making perfect, sharp points is to be sure the excess fabric has been trimmed before turning under seam allowance. Remember, all the excess fabric has to fit under that tiny point and if there is too much, the point will be round and lumpy.

Fray-Free Inverted Points. Before pinning the appliqué piece to background fabric, clip through the seam allowance to the pencil-marked point, making sure to clip all the way to the pencil line. As you stitch toward the inverted point, such as the center of a heart, place appliqué stitches closer together. Two stitches from the point, turn the whole quilt block so that appliqué will progress in the proper direction after point is stitched.

In preparation for taking the next few stitches, turn under the seam allowance on the other side of the inverted point. Next, using needle as a tool, smooth under with a sweeping motion any stray threads that may be protruding from the inverted point. Needle will move between background fabric and appliqué piece to make the "sweep."

When satisfied that all stray threads are tucked under, take the next stitch or two toward the point. The center stitch (in the point) is made by taking a deep stitch. On all other appliqué stitches, only a small "bite" is taken from the edge of the fold. This stitch is made by bringing needle up several threads (4–5 threads) inside the point. Continue stitch, placing point of needle underneath the edge of the appliqué motif (needle point will be out of view) and go down through the background fabric, right next to where needle came up, for the deep stitch. Finish stitch by moving needle horizontally underneath background fabric to take next stitch and proceed as normal. This deep stitch creates a tuck that pulls all of the fraying threads under and holds them in place.

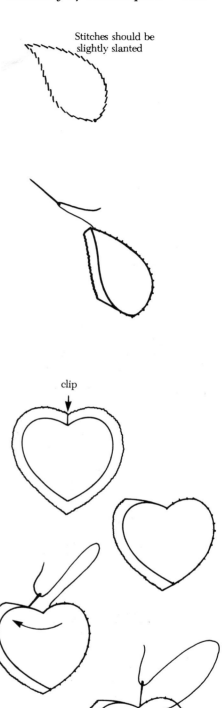

Stitches should be slightly slanted

clip

Cutting Away Back of Appliqué. Cutting away the background fabric will make a big difference in the finished block. Separate the appliqué from the background fabric, then snip the background fabric just enough to slide the scissors inside. Trim ¼" from the edge, using the stitches as a guide. This will make the appliqué lie flatter and eliminate the possibility of having to quilt through extra layers of fabric.

Do not cut away background fabric until you are certain the appliqué piece is positioned correctly. When several layers of appliqué are used, cut away each background layer before appliquéing the next layer.

Perfect Circle Construction

Circles are a problem in appliqué because it is difficult to begin and finish stitching on a curve while keeping the curve smooth. This method was developed to assist in keeping all edges smooth and round.

1. Make a stiff plastic template the actual size of the finished circle. This template is used in the stitching of the circle. It is extremely important that the template be a perfect circle; the finished product is dependent upon the shape of the plastic template. (It is helpful to use a circle template, which can be purchased at office supply stores, to draw the circle perfectly.)

2. Make a template for cutting fabric that is twice as big as the actual size circle template. For example, a ½" diameter circle requires a 1" diameter circle cut from fabric. **Note:** There are two separate templates required for this method, one cut from stiff plastic and one that is used to mark and cut fabric.

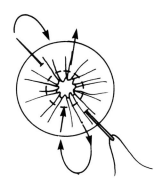

3. Using matching thread that has been knotted, baste ⅛" from raw edges around fabric circle (there are no pencil markings on fabric). After basting is complete, place plastic template inside circle and pull thread; plastic is now encased inside fabric.

4. Without tying a knot, or cutting thread, stitch back and forth across circle through the gathers, as if making the spokes of a wagon wheel. This step pulls any possible bumps or peaks away from the outside edge, leaving a perfect, smooth edge to stitch down. Don't be concerned about removing the plastic template; it will be removed in the last step. Cut the thread.

5. Position circle into its proper place and hold firmly in place while appliquéing with small stitches. Be sure to take stitches on the edge of circle only, catching a few threads with each stitch. After circle is appliquéd into place, tie knot on wrong side of background fabric.

6. On wrong side of background fabric, use scissors with a strong, sharp point to cut down through background fabric and excess gathered fabric, until scissors touch plastic template. Cut out a small circle, leaving at least ⅛" seam allowance to reveal the plastic circle inside. Remove plastic by sliding out, as if unbuttoning a button. The plastic is now ready to be used in the next circle.

Alternate Perfect Circle Method

Some of the circles in these patterns are used as flower centers, or they overlap previous appliqué stitching lines. When this occurs, I recommend using the following circle construction method:

1. Follow steps 1–3 for the Perfect Circle Construction technique, with the exception of using the plastic template. Instead, cut template from stiff cardboard, such as a manila folder.
2. After drawing up basting thread, tie a knot and cut thread.
3. Press the circle firmly with a hot iron.
4. Remove basting thread and cardboard template.
5. Trim excess fabric as necessary and appliqué into place along pressed edge.

To make padded or stuffed cherries, place a very small amount of stuffing inside basted fabric before inserting plastic template. When plastic is removed, the stuffing stays in place, because seam allowance holds it there. Crisscross stitches may be taken to form a web that holds stuffing in, but care must be taken to make these stitches loose, since the cherry can be distorted if stitches are pulled tight.

Bias-Strip Construction

A $^3/_8$" bias is used throughout this book.

1. Cut fabric on the bias $1^1/_4$" wide and the required length.
2. Place wrong sides together and use either hand or sewing machine basting stitches to sew bias strip together lengthwise with a scant $^1/_4$" seam allowance.
3. Press bias strip flat, making sure seam allowance is pressed to back of strip. (Seam allowance will be hidden under bias strip when it is appliquéd down.)

Reverse Appliqué

Reverse, or overlaid, appliqué is a technique in which an upper layer of fabric is cut and turned back to expose a lower layer of fabric. The projects in this book use reverse appliqué to add detail on several of the blocks.

1. Prepare upper layer of fabric as usual for appliqué. Mark areas where upper layer will be opened up to expose lower layer.
2. Cut lower layer of fabric the exact size of actual size pattern; do not add seam allowances.
3. Layer upper fabric piece over lower piece and pin into place. Appliqué all around upper piece as described in Needle-Turn Appliqué instructions on pages 151–54. The lower layer is now encased by upper layer and is not visible.

4. Carefully cut along center of marked area. Clip sparingly, as needed, along concave areas.
5. Needle-turn and appliqué raw edges under to expose lower fabric.

Light Box

Light boxes can be purchased from office or architectural supply stores, but they are expensive. The following is an inexpensive alternative that achieves the same result:

Separate your dining room table as if adding an extra leaf. Place a piece of glass, plastic, or Plexiglas™ in the opening. (I have used the removable glass from a screen door.) Set a table lamp on the floor underneath the glass and you have an instant light table.

The glass, plastic, or Plexiglas™ can be purchased at a glass store and cut to fit your table, if desired.

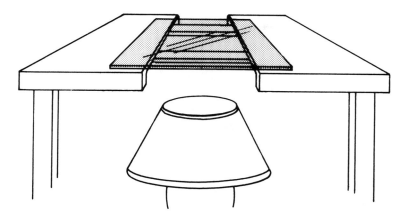

Bibliography

Bank, Mirra. *Anonymous Was a Woman.* New York: St. Martin's Press, 1979.

Barber, Rita Barrow. *Somewhere in Between Quilts and Quilters of Illinois.* Paducah, Kentucky: American Quilters Society, 1986.

Bath, Virginia Churchill. *Needlework in America.* New York: The Viking Press, 1979.

Binney III, Edwin, and Binney-Winslow, Gail. *Homage to Amanda: Two Hundred Years of American Quilts.* San Francisco: R K Press, 1984.

Bishop, Robert. *New Discoveries in American Quilts.* New York: E. P. Dutton, 1975.

_____. *Quilts, Coverlets, Rugs and Samplers.* New York: Alfred A. Knopf, 1982.

Bishop, Robert, and Houck, Carter. *All Flags Flying.* New York: E. P. Dutton, 1986.

Brackman, Barbara. *American Patchwork Quilt.* Tokyo, Japan: Spencer Museum of Art and Kokusai Art, 1987.

_____. "Clues in the Calico." *Quilter's Newsletter Magazine* (October 1989), pp. 42–44.

Bresenhan, Karoline Patterson, and Puentes, Nancy O'Bryant. *Lone Stars: A Legacy of Texas Quilts, 1836–1936.* Austin, Texas: University of Texas Press, 1986.

Bullard, Lacy Folmar, and Shiell, Betty Jo. *Chintz Quilts: Unfading Glory.* Tallahassee, Florida: Serendipity Publishers, 1983.

Carter, Kate B. "Trees, Flowers and Birds of Utah." *Heart Throbs of the West,* Vol. 2. Salt Lake City: Daughters of Utah Pioneers, 1940.

_____. "Pioneer Quilts." *Our Pioneer Heritage,* Vol. 18., Salt Lake City: Daughters of Utah Pioneers, 1975.

Cincinnati Art Museum. *Quilts from Cincinnati Collections.* Cincinnati, Ohio: Cincinnati Art Museum, 1985.

Euliss, E. S., ed. *Alamance County: The Legacy of Its People and Places.* Greensboro, North Carolina: Legacy Publications, 1984.

Finley, Ruth E. *Old Patchwork Quilts and the Women Who Made Them.* Newton Center, Massachusetts: Charles T. Branford Company, 1929.

Fox, Sandi. *Quilts in Utah: A Reflection of the Western Experience.* Salt Lake City: Salt Lake Arts Center, 1981.

_____. *19th Century American Patchwork.* Tokyo, Japan: The Seibu Museum of Art, 1983.

_____. *Small Endearments.* New York: Charles Scribner's Sons, 1985.

Haders, Phyllis. *The Warner Collector's Guide to American Quilts.* New York: The Main Street Press, 1981.

Hall, Carrie A., and Kretsinger, Rose G. *The Romance of the Patchwork Quilt in America.* New York: Bonanza Books, 1935.

Havig, Bettina. *Missouri Heritage Quilts.* Paducah, Kentucky: American Quilter's Society, 1986.

Holstein, Jonathan. *The Pieced Quilt.* Boston: Little, Brown and Company, 1973.

Holstein, Jonathan and Finley, John,. *Kentucky Quilts 1800–1900.* Louisville, Kentucky: The Kentucky Quilt Project, Inc., 1982.

Ickis, Marguerite. *The Standard Book of Quiltmaking and Collecting.* New York: Dover Publications, Inc., 1959.

Keyser, Alan G. "Beds, Bedding, Bedsteads and Sleep." *Pieced By Mother Symposium Papers.* Lewisburg, Pennsylvania: Oral Traditions Project of Union County Historical Society, 1988.

Kiracofe, Roderick. "Showcase." *The Quilt Digest* (1984), pp. 34–57.

_____. "Showcase." *The Quilt Digest* (1985), pp. 36–59.

Kirkpatrick, Erma Hughes. "Garden Variety Appliqué." *North Carolina Quilts.* Chapel Hill, North Carolina: The University of North Carolina Press, 1988.

Lasansky, Jeannette. *In the Heart of Pennsylvania.* Lewisburg, Pennsylvania: Oral Traditions Project of Union County Historical Society, 1985.

_____. *Pieced By Mother.* Lewisburg, Pennsylvania: Oral Traditions Project of Union County Historical Society, 1987.

Lockley, Fred. *Conversations with Pioneer Women.* Eugene, Oregon: Rainy Day Press, 1981.

MacDowell, Marsha, and Fitzgerald, Ruth D. *Michigan Quilts: 150 Years of a Textile Tradition.* East Lansing, Michigan: Michigan State University Museum, 1987.

Martin, Nancy J. *Pieces of the Past.* Bothell, Washington: That Patchwork Place, Inc., 1986.

McCloskey, Marsha. *Christmas Quilts.* Bothell, Washington: That Patchwork Place, Inc., 1985.

Nelson, Cyril I., and Houck, Carter. *The Quilt Engagement Calendar Treasury.* New York: E. P. Dutton, 1982.

Orlofsky, Patsy and Myron. *Quilts in America.* New York: McGraw-Hill Book Company, 1974.

Ramsey, Bets, and Waldvogel, Merikay. *The Quilts of Tennessee: Images of Domestic Life Prior to 1930.* Nashville, Tennessee: Rutledge Hill Press, 1986.

Safford, Carleton L., and Bishop, Robert. *America's Quilts and Coverlets.* New York: E. P. Dutton, 1980.

Snow, Bess, and Beckstrom, Elizabeth S. *O' Ye Mountains High: The Story of Pine Valley.* St. George, Utah: Heritage Press, 1980.

Stewart, Elinore Pruitt. *Letters on an Elk Hunt.* Lincoln, Nebraska: University of Nebraska Press, 1915.

Strasser, Susan. *Never Done: A History of American Housework.* New York: Pantheon Books, 1982.

Swan, Susan Burrows. "Quiltmaking Within Women's Repertoire." *In the Heart of Pennsylvania Symposium Papers.* Lewisburg, Pennsylvania: Oral Traditions Project of Union County Historical Society, 1986.

Woodard, Thomas K., and Greenstein, Blanche. *Crib Quilts and Other Small Wonders.* New York: E. P. Dutton, 1981.

Notes

1. Susan Burrows Swan, "Quiltmaking Within Women's Repertoire," *In the Heart of Pennsylvania Symposium Papers,* p. 8.
2. Mirra Bank, *Anonymous Was a Woman,* p. 23.
3. Susan Strasser, *Never Done,* p. 131.
4. Patsy and Myron Orlofsky, *Quilts in America,* pp. 26–27.
5. Jeannette Lasansky, *In the Heart of Pennsylvania,* p. 27.
6. Marguerite Ickis, *The Standard Book of Quiltmaking and Collecting,* p. 259.
7. Ruth E. Finley, *Old Patchwork Quilts and the Women Who Made Them,* pp. 127–128.
8. Kate B. Carter, *Heart Throbs of the West,* p. 19.
9. Orlofsky, *Quilts in America,* p. 6.
10. Ibid.
11. Jonathan Holstein, *The Pieced Quilt,* pp. 15–18.
12. Lacy Folmar Bullard and Betty Jo Shiell, *Chintz Quilts,* p. 12.
13. Holstein, *The Pieced Quilt,* p. 18.
14. Ibid., pp. 18–19.
15. Virginia Churchill Bath, *Needlework in America,* p. 88.
16. Alan G. Keyser, "Beds, Bedding, Bedsteads and Sleep," *Pieced By Mother Symposium Papers,* p. 24.
17. Swan, "Quiltmaking within Women's Repertoire," p. 13.
18. Ibid.
19. Erma Hughes Kirkpatrick, "Garden Variety Appliqué," *North Carolina Quilts,* p. 81.
20. Orlofsky, *Quilts in America,* p. 35.
21. Barbara Brackman, "Clues in the Calico," *Quilter's Newsletter Magazine,* October 1989, p. 44.
22. Ibid.
23. Carrie A. Hall and Rose G. Kretsinger, *The Romance of the Patchwork Quilt in America,* pp. 34–35.
24. Kate B. Carter, "Pioneer Quilts," *Our Pioneer Heritage,* p. 81.
25. Finley, *Old Patchwork Quilts and the Women Who Made Them,* pp. 193–94.
26. Ibid., p. 111.
27. The three Cotton Boll quilts can be seen in *Arkansas Quilts,* p. 143, and in *North Carolina Quilts,* pp. 92 and 94 (the quilt shown on p. 94 is also pictured in *Lady's Circle Patchwork Quilts,* No. 20, on p. 20). Interestingly, there is a border on a Rose Wreath quilt that uses the Cotton Boll design. It can be seen on p. 10 of *Quilting U.S.A.* magazine, No. 9.
28. Finley, *Old Patchwork Quilts and the Women Who Made Them,* p. 133.
29. The other Pineapple Carnation quilts can be seen in *Kentucky Quilts,* p. 24 and *Quilts in America,* p. 318; *Needlework in America,* p. 222, pictures a quilted counterpane (c. 1800–1820) that includes the same design elements as part of its stuffed work motifs.
30. Marguerite Ickis, *The Standard Book of Quiltmaking and Collecting,* p. 54.

Martingale & Company
Toll-free: 1-800-426-3126

International: 1-425-483-3313
24-Hour Fax: 1-425-486-7596

PO Box 118, Bothell, WA 98041-0118 USA

Web site: www.patchwork.com
E-mail: info@martingale-pub.com

Books from

These books are available through your local quilt, fabric, craft-supply, or art-supply store. For more information, contact us for a free full-color catalog. You can also find our full catalog of books online at www.patchwork.com.

Appliqué

Appliqué for Baby
Appliqué in Bloom
Baltimore Bouquets
Basic Quiltmaking Techniques for Hand Appliqué
Basic Quiltmaking Techniques for Machine Appliqué
Coxcomb Quilt
The Easy Art of Appliqué
Folk Art Animals
Fun with Sunbonnet Sue
Garden Appliqué
The Nursery Rhyme Quilt
Red and Green: An Appliqué Tradition
Rose Sampler Supreme
Stars in the Garden
Sunbonnet Sue All Through the Year

Beginning Quiltmaking

Basic Quiltmaking Techniques for Borders & Bindings
Basic Quiltmaking Techniques for Curved Piecing
Basic Quiltmaking Techniques for Divided Circles
Basic Quiltmaking Techniques for Eight-Pointed Stars
Basic Quiltmaking Techniques for Hand Appliqué
Basic Quiltmaking Techniques for Machine Appliqué
Basic Quiltmaking Techniques for Strip Piecing
The Quilter's Handbook
Your First Quilt Book (or it should be!)

Crafts

15 Beads
Fabric Mosaics
Folded Fabric Fun
Making Memories

Cross-Stitch & Embroidery

Hand-Stitched Samplers from I Done My Best
Kitties to Stitch and Quilt: 15 Redwork Designs
Miniature Baltimore Album Quilts
A Silk-Ribbon Album

Designing Quilts

Color: The Quilter's Guide
Design Essentials: The Quilter's Guide
Design Your Own Quilts
Designing Quilts: The Value of Value
The Nature of Design
QuiltSkills
Sensational Settings
Surprising Designs from Traditional Quilt Blocks
Whimsies & Whynots

Holiday

Christmas Ribbonry
Easy Seasonal Wall Quilts
Favorite Christmas Quilts from That Patchwork Place
Holiday Happenings
Quilted for Christmas
Quilted for Christmas, Book IV
Special-Occasion Table Runners
Welcome to the North Pole

Home Decorating

The Home Decorator's Stamping Book
Make Room for Quilts
Special-Occasion Table Runners
Stitch & Stencil
Welcome Home: Debbie Mumm
Welcome Home: Kaffe Fassett

Knitting

Simply Beautiful Sweaters
Two Sticks and a String

Paper Arts

The Art of Handmade Paper and Collage
Grow Your Own Paper
Stamp with Style

Paper Piecing

Classic Quilts with Precise Foundation Piecing
Easy Machine Paper Piecing
Easy Mix & Match Machine Paper Piecing
Easy Paper-Pieced Keepsake Quilts
Easy Paper-Pieced Miniatures
Easy Reversible Vests
Go Wild with Quilts
Go Wild with Quilts—Again!
It's Raining Cats & Dogs
Mariner's Medallion
Needles and Notions
Paper-Pieced Curves
Paper Piecing the Seasons
A Quilter's Ark
Sewing on the Line
Show Me How to Paper Piece

Quilting & Finishing Techniques

The Border Workbook
Borders by Design
A Fine Finish
Happy Endings
Interlacing Borders
Lap Quilting Lives!
Loving Stitches
Machine Quilting Made Easy
Quilt It!
Quilting Design Sourcebook
Quilting Makes the Quilt
The Ultimate Book of Quilt Labels

Ribbonry

Christmas Ribbonry
A Passion for Ribbonry
Wedding Ribbonry

Rotary Cutting & Speed Piecing

101 Fabulous Rotary-Cut Quilts
365 Quilt Blocks a Year Perpetual Calendar
All-Star Sampler
Around the Block with Judy Hopkins
Basic Quiltmaking Techniques for Strip Piecing
Beyond Log Cabin
Block by Block
Easy Stash Quilts
Fat Quarter Quilts
The Joy of Quilting
A New Twist on Triangles
A Perfect Match
Quilters on the Go
ScrapMania
Shortcuts
Simply Scrappy Quilts
Spectacular Scraps
Square Dance
Stripples Strikes Again!
Strips That Sizzle
Surprising Designs from Traditional Quilt Blocks

Traditional Quilts with Painless Borders
Time-Crunch Quilts
Two-Color Quilts

Small & Miniature Quilts

Bunnies by the Bay Meets Little Quilts
Celebrate! With Little Quilts
Easy Paper-Pieced Miniatures
Fun with Miniature Log Cabin Blocks
Little Quilts all Through the House
Living with Little Quilts
Miniature Baltimore Album Quilts
A Silk-Ribbon Album
Small Quilts Made Easy
Small Wonders

Surface Design

Complex Cloth
Creative Marbling on Fabric
Dyes & Paints
Fantasy Fabrics
Hand-Dyed Fabric Made Easy
Jazz It Up
Machine Quilting with Decorative Threads
New Directions in Chenille
Thread Magic
Threadplay with Libby Lehman

Topics in Quiltmaking

Bargello Quilts
The Cat's Meow
Even More Quilts for Baby
Everyday Angels in Extraordinary Quilts
Fabric Collage Quilts
Fast-and-Fun Stenciled Quilts
Folk Art Quilts
It's Raining Cats & Dogs
Kitties to Stitch and Quilt: 15 Redwork Designs
Life in the Country with Country Threads
Machine-Stitched Cathedral Windows
More Quilts for Baby
A New Slant on Bargello Quilts
Patchwork Pantry
Pink Ribbon Quilts
Quilted Landscapes
The Quilted Nursery
Quilting Your Memories
Quilts for Baby
Quilts from Aunt Amy
Whimsies & Whynots

Watercolor Quilts

More Strip-Pieced Watercolor Magic
Quick Watercolor Quilts
Strip-Pieced Watercolor Magic
Watercolor Impressions
Watercolor Quilts

Wearables

Easy Reversible Vests
Just Like Mommy
New Directions in Chenille
Quick-Sew Fleece
Variations in Chenille